The Prairie Was Home

by Pauline Neher Diede

Pauline N. Diede

"The Prairie Was Home' is an account of 'Paulie' Neher's life, written by herself, of life on the prairie ... from 1916 to 1936.

As she roamed the stony hills, with their treachery and treasures, she gained the basis for life's education and attained a 'faith' in the Creator-God ... "I lift my eyes to the hills. My help comes from the Lord who made heaven and earth!" Psalm 121.

** TO HIM BE THE GLORY ! **

****

Printed under the auspices of John H. Gengler by the Abbey Press, Richardton, North Dakota 58652.

****

Special art for this book was created by Hebron artist James Mische, who teaches art and mathematics at Richardton-Taylor High School.

ACKNOWLEDGEMENTS

To the Knife River/Elm Creek area friends, I exclaim, "Remember when?!"

To the memory of my parents, Ludwig and Christina Neher, who tamed the prairieland and settled their children in the greatest country--USA, I pay heartfelt tribute!

To my sisters and brother: Matilda, Ottilia, Elsie, Louise, Edwin, Anne and Clara, I recognize with love!

To my children, grandchildren and great-grandchildren, I advocate a challenge for life and bequeath a faith in the Creator-God!

****

COPYRIGHT 1986 by Pauline Neher Diede. Printed in the United States. All rights reserved. Except for brief quotations in critical articles and reviews, no part of this book may be reproduced in any form or by any means, electronic or mechanical, including photocopying or recording; or by any information storage or retrieval system, movie, dramatic, television, motion or talking picture purposes without the authorization from the holder of these rights without permission in writing from Pauline Neher Diede, Box 108, Hebron ND 58638 (or her son, Rod Diede, Bowman, ND 58623); nor can anyone sell my books without paying royalty to the holder of this book.

A NOTE FROM EDITOR JOHN H. GENGLER

Pauline Neher Diede has captured the spirit of what it was like to grow up on the prairies of North Dakota as a child of one of many among the German-Russian families who came to this isolated part of America at the turn of the century. She shares her heart and soul with her readers, describing hundreds of experiences which were common to children then, from eating and sleeping with a home full o siblings, to enjoying Nature as only a child can enjoy it.

Her insight into the traditional, strongly religious mind of the German-Russian immigrants tells us much of who these hard-working people were and why they insisted on staying and taming this treeless prairieland.

We owe Pauline a debt of gratitude for letting us see into her innermost being, for sharing her sorrows and joys, and for teaching us about the God-fearing men and women whose industrious spirit conquered the prairies. More than one-fourth of North Dakota's population come from this stock, and because Pauline ha passed on these treasures of that German-Russian heritage, those of us from that lineage can better know who we are and thus carry on in the same spirit.

(John H. Gengler has spent his entire life in Stark County, growing up in Dickinson, attending school at Assumption Abbey in Richardton, graduating from DSC, teaching at South Heart, serving as Director of Public Relations at Assumption College, with the last 16 years spent as principal and American government teacher at Richardton High School. He was co-founder and co-editor of the Richardton Merchant, edited the Richardton Centennial book, and also edited Pauline Diede's "Speaking-Out-On Sod-House Times" book.

PAULINE
NEHER
DIEDE

THE AUTHOR

Pauline Neher Diede is a native of North Dakota, a sod-house product, born on Oct. 10, 1911, the third of eight children of Ludwig and Christina Neher, homesteaders and immigrants from South Russia.

She grew up in an undeveloped, stony-hills-country. She graduated from Elm Creek country school, Model High and from a secretarial course at Dickinson Normal School.

She married Jake Diede and raised and educated three children, Darlayne, Audrey and Rodney, with a country-life environment. She was affiliated with newspaper features and columns for 25 years and wrote her first book, Homesteading on the Knife River Prairies, in 1983. This, her third book, The Prairie Was Home, is a sequel to the Homesteading book. The publication of Speaking-out on Sod House Times, her second book, was a compilation of interviews with sod-house pioneers. The Prairie Was Home describes the author's life on the open prairieland, a tear-rending as well as an amusing account of the years 1916 to 1936.

4

TABLE OF CONTENTS

THE PRAIRIE WAS HOME
Introductions
Pages 1-9

THE HOMESTEAD
Prairie's Innocence
Page 10

THE FARMSTEAD
Prairie's Range
Page 59

THE ROARING TWENTIES
Prairie's Generosity
Page 99

THE DIRTY THIRTIES
Prairie's Salutation
Page 143

A SPECIAL SECTION
Page 148

FOREWORD

Frontier times on the wide, open and wild prairie lands were phenomenal and alien for the immigrant settlers. No following generation can comprehend the isolating nature the pioneers faced. This world was strange and new ... an endless sea of sculptured surface and an eery vastness.

The Great Glacier had done its sorting in a characterizing manner, leaving a distinct landscape of variant lay-outs. Rolling and table-flat hills were dotted with prairie stones. Forked ravines with tree-bush cover leading into a creek that coursed into a river. Valleys and stretches of level land. Buttes that silhouetted the horizons with a mysterious outline. The sunrises and sunsets cast an ever-changing wonderment. This dire-point of the unknown was to be tamed.

Immigrants from European countries and from the eastern United States were challenged by the two words---"free land"! Here was free opportunity for a home on 'My Land'! Here was the unwritten rule that fate had it for a good future. And here-upon adversity, the notion of fear must not be pondered on, even if the world appeared stark.

There was no Land-Extension material, no newspaper or magazine to learn from. (Far removed yet were the telephone, radio and television.) The Bible was the pioneer-man's only written matter from which he gathered wisdom and strength for the day-to-day encounters.

The pioneer likewise pitted knowledge from animal ways, weather and Nature's signs. And they practiced the historically ethnic-people's manner of know-how. Even their reasoning proved right from great-grandfather's word. They seemed to have a trust beyond human analysis. It was meant by divine order for them to challenge the grotesque prairielands!

The pioneer watched animal technique. It was evident that wild animals could show some way of refuge for survival. Something like a coyote, digging a hole into the earth, rounding it out and making a staid abode for her young. So the human settler scooped out an earthen-home on the side of a suitable bank or hill. Or, with prairieland stones and sod he shaped a one-room home --- the most common home of the early pioneers --- the sod house.

By instinct, the coyote howled, connoting hunger and that wily animal would prey upon anything to feed her young and herself; whereas the settler would pray to God, the Provider, to render him the power to think and do for the next step to sustenance. The Bible, which housed the soul of man, was the pioneer's extension-material ... the Word for courage, work, and hope that Nature's wild prairieland would relent to taming to provide sufficiently for the day. And more generously for the future. Prayer substantiated!

IN FOCUS

Slowly I walk from one earth-indent to the other where nearly four-score years ago my immigrant-parents settled on the wild prairieland of southwest Mercer County, North Dakota, USA, by the bend of the Knife River (eighteen miles north of the town of Hebron and fourteen miles south of Golden Valley).

On this beautiful late summer afternoon (August, 1985) I squat by the homestead premise where once stood a one-room rugged abode. It was made out of the prairie's virgin sod-slabs. These were layered in a staggered manner and shaped to a rectangular. The very frontier dwelling place.

Here was a sample of the many stone re-enforced and sod-made shelters ... made to house man or animal, not so much different in plan or design. Just something that afforded protection from the forces of Nature. So to maintain life.

Ludwig and Christina Neher and their first child immigrated from South Russia to America during the autumn season of 1909 and wintered in a train box-car in Ashley, ND. Then in the spring of 1910 they settled on a homestead just as thousands of other immigrants had done over the vast undeveloped plains.

"The Prairie Was Home" is an autobiography directly following the biographical story: "Homesteading on the Knife River Prairie" (1816-1916) featuring the Neher and Martin families and representing the ethnic-people of Germans from Russia. The various nationality-settlers join the picture of the fascinating accounts of homesteading.

The two books are sequels.

"The Prairie Was Home" is an account of the author's life beginning at her childhood, approximately at the age of nearly five years, as impressions registered.

The family lived in a rectangular sod-constructed room with a newly lumber-made kitchen attached to the west side of the sod-abode (1916).

Included in the Neher family were Dadee (Ludwig), Momee (Christina), Dilda (Matilda, born in 1907 in South Russia), Odeela (Ottilia, born enroute to the homestead in America, 1910), Paulie (Pauline, first to be born in an earthen-floor sod-room, 1911), Elza (Elsie, 1913), Louiza (Louise, 1914).

The story begins with five little girls and parents housed in one sleeping room and a kitchen. The language was German. Definitely. The traditional Swabian German sufficed in the Neher home, pertaining to the pride of Germany.

The story centers around Elm Creek District 21 where a variety of nationality immigrants homesteaded: German, Irish, English, Hungarians, Norwegians and likely others. Each nationality spoke the homeland language in the beginning. Therefore, the low-German language in this story rules definitely.

- 3 0 -

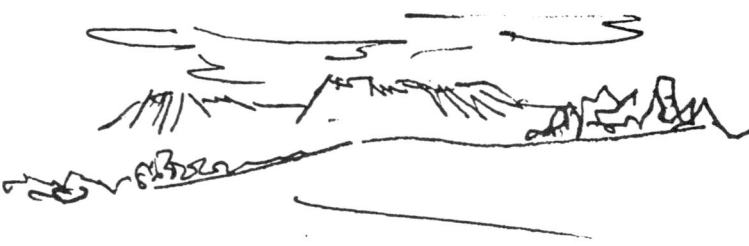

The Homestead
Prairie's Innocence

It was summertime. There was a thundershower during the night and droplets of water were still dripping outside the sod-house window. Blob. Blob. Then it stopped a bit. It had been a few hours since the downpour and the dribble gradually lessened. The morning's sun rays touched the tardy droplets and memory marks a glitter. I had been sucking soaked bread, which was pressed and tied into a lump on a cloth corner. Intentionally Momee made up the node to take the place of a pacifier.

The need for sucking on something during the night times was quite prevalent among pioneer children. In our primitive home was no exception. Every child was offered a suck-node, mainly to quiet them down. After all, five little girls and a set of parents, all sleeping in one room, incurs disturbance. Obviously, due to malnutrition or discomfort, crying or wailing denoted a need. How could Momee and Dadee get rest? Especially Momee.

The three of us older girlies slept on the splintery-board floor. The mattress-type ticking was filled with soft, dry foliage and for every move there was a rustle. The cloth-case was of a faded gray, where, fastened onto its top corners were tied two lumps which Dilda and Odeela could suck on. But my node was tied onto a separate cloth since I slept in the middle. We did have two massive feather-filled pillows, so soft and soothing, though often causing wheezing (allergy tendencies to sensitive children at this point in medical science were still remote).

Wide awake this particular morning, I heard Elza suck. Its sound resembled a draw for which reason I became restless. Quietly I crept out from the floor bed much too early in the morning. Elza slept in a kind of a man-made box-crib and the one-year-old Louiza laid at any spot on the only bed there was. Here Momee and Dadee slept. The tightly-wrapped Louiza child wailed in prolonged sounds, naturally from the discomforts of the tightness. Elza sucked and moaned as if hungry. Kin-rivalry where the three slept took place rather frequently. The acts of kicking each other because of a too-close body-rub. Or, for the pull of a cover.

I crawled out carefully and scanned over to the deep inset of a small window where the warm morning light shone in. I reached for Nature's glittering droplet which had clung to a trailing prairie vine. As of a child's curiosity, certain to test if it was for a real feel of a 'schternle' (star). The plant had climbed and crept through the crevice next to the window frame and trailed down into thin air where the rain-droplet stayed.

At that moment Momee came in from the shanty-kitchen where she brewed coffee with 'zigori' and had cooked the oatmeal for Dadee's breakfast. She caught me fingering the vine, and in a low tone of voice, chided and shooed me back to bed. The impression fixed. Open-eyed I gazed at the vine with interest to get back at it again. Curiosity of every growing thing and the feel of plants and animals was an apt and natural inclination. In the vine's wonderment I sensed a delight in the midst of kin restlessness.

I had tender feelings for anything alive and suffered right with any animal or bird that was exposed to hurt. To see a bird dangle on a dog's mouth, or see a rabbit hunted down, or a horse whipped by an irate man caused me emotional upset ... so much that when the cruelty took place I would hide in a huddle, either behind a large stone by a hill, or lean against a sod barn-wall to cry. With my hand holding onto the protruding part of a sod and in another moment using the same fist to rub my weepy eyes, likely ejecting the dirt-element into my right eye. What excruciating pain! I ran to Momee. There wasn't much accomplished to soothe the pain. Momee was not handy at any nursing act!

The irritation inflamed to the point where Dadee had to take me to Mutter Boehler during the night and luckily she managed to get the sticker out; then the elder woman dabbed the swollen eye with herb-tea. Of course the "brauching" (divine soothing) performance was a must. Momee believed religiously in the act of "brauching". It seemed it was her human trust to rely on the elder-mothers for "brauching".

In the process of Mother Boehler's treatment she removed her sole-worn shoe and pressed the sole-press had anything to do with the effect of a cure, as I later pondered, I doubt; however, the Physician Above to do His part. Whether the sole-press had anything to do with effect of a cure, as I later pondered, I doubt; however, the divine-connected practice remains an aid to healing by way of faith. At the time I felt securely good, whatever the merciful Grandmother did. The pain eased and the swelling went down.

Being of a curious nature and not much for fore-warning, I became a victim prone to suffer through many mishaps. Nature's lessons had to be learned by way of distress. Much too often I would be hurt, then I'd find a place to cry it out. My best solace sought Nature's animation and the animal realm. It could be a warm stone where I sat on or laid near it during the period of physical or mental hurt. The balm of the stone's gentle warmth restored a soothing influence.

It could be the chirp of a sparrow or the call of a meadowlark perched on a post that cheered; so the cottontail would suddenly hop by at close range and charge me to an onrush for investigation where her nest might be. I'd settle to do that rather than to nurture the agony of the hurt. It was as if I was born to be a tamer of prairieland creatures.

Dog "Beller" was our first homestead-yard dog. I can describe him as bedraggled, long-haired, with brownish colored covering and white spots that were hardly white. The word 'beller' in German meant 'barker'. Most of the time he was half-starved, just as I was. Beller's survival depended mainly on his catch: mice, young rabbits or sniffing out the young, naked birdies from a nest, or prior to that, its eggs.

The pair of elder-birds acted out a ferocious immitation flutter and cried out lamenting sounds to distract the dog away from the nest. How the bird-pair could figure out such a pretentious trickery act for protecting their young proves the family instinct ... a common impulse for amiable safety, even with animals.

As Beller grew older and wiser, he became the threat to birds' nests. I scolded as I pulled his tail and cried along with the bird-pair after another nest had been molested. At one time I lashed at him with a switch. Beller only pulled in his tail, ran astride with drooped ears, pitifully gazing at me as if to say he did it because of hunger. I must have forgiven him again and again for I needed to cuddle close to him when I was tired, and rightly Beller complied. He would slither close to me, then sniff and lie down ... a clue for a need for my closeness. The furry warmth of a dog and the shrieking cry of a pair of meadowlarks spelled utter confusion in a child's mind. Awhile before lying down Beller again had devoured the three baby birds in a rather secluded nest. I listened to the mournful cry with a declining moan of the bird-pair, and finally one day they left the prairie premises for good. There was no need to cleave to stricken grounds. I could not comprehend why animals had to hurt birds.

Beller's life was at stake. He had discovered even an easier seize for eats as he detected the chicken coop nests and began to snatch an egg, one by one. To kill a dog for such misdeeds was very much a part of any homesteader's decisive doings. There were no two ways about it. When the family was denied eggs for food as well as for marketing, to get rid of the preyer was the alternative. A common German saying tested it's truth: "der isch ko-ie schusz bulfer wert!" ("he is not worth a gun shot")! But it took a gunshot to get rid of Beller. What a hurting and undergoing of intense suffering I went through. I sorely missed Beller.

Since the dog and cat life was on the open range, the litters multiplied fast. It was not hard to replace a dog. Two or three pups from a neighbor were easily adopted with little thought for feed, it seemed. Table scraps were hardly enough for several dogs and the skim milk had to be rationed for the pail-calves and other farm animals. The hunger of dogs, cats or any of the prairie-creatures remained a life-time plague for me.

Desperately homesick for Beller on this hot summer day I wandered about the north-hill naturally longing for another animal-friend. As even the favorite meadowlark pair had flown away, I sobbed and sniffed and stumbled back to the shady part of the north side of the sod-house, a favorite retreat. I laid down and fell asleep. Upon awakening and sitting up I beheld a slender reptile close by. After rubbing my eyes to see clearer, I noticed the green and yellow stripes of a visitor. I stretched out my hand and touched it. It was alive and crawling about. Could it be that I'd found a new animal friend? The snake sizzled about, making a hissing sound. I carried on a conversation as I often had with Beller and with the larks. The snake coiled and stuck its head upward, sticking out its tongue as though it wanted to respond, either in charge or as a crony. I liked that. For a homesick child this did my being good. So I talked quite loudly!

At that moment Momee appeared and as she saw a snake so close to me, she screamed at the top of her voice. The snake slithered along the sod-wall around the northeast corner and disappeared. Momee then grabbed and botched (spanked) me .... then in lieu of consolation and understanding, I cried loudly and vehemently. Hurt and angry because of another might-have-been friend had been denied me. I felt no danger in this colorful and twisting animal.

Momee treated all of her little girls with acute anguish ... scolded as well as disciplined with unreserved thrusts. She never dealt easily with animals and never took to Prairieland's creatures. There was relentless fear of preying animals, like the coyote or the overhead hawk that snatched a chick from a week-old hatch; or, from a rebellious bull, she would scream. Even moreso Momee would react with great fear to any kind of a crawling creature, such as a snake, lizard or even worms. She'd have hysteria! Ants, flies or crickets she detested. Such aversion toward living creatures created a definite incompatibility between her and me. Since I felt an innate closeness to Prairieland life, a certain fervor for outdoor adventure ruled my young life.

The garden-snake reappeared at the sod-lodge ... the reptile vanished alright after the outbreak of disorder on the shady spot of the soddy yester-afternoon. It fissured into a sod-layer for a good repose. The next morning at daybreak Dadee arose from the bed intently stepping on the gunney-rug and immediately felt a weird kind of movement on the bottom of one foot. He knew directly it wasn't a healthy foot-massage. It was 'the snake' coiled under the comforts of a gunney. Without hesitation Dadee wrapped the invader into a coarse bundle, grabbed it and rushed outdoors where it received its doom. Dadee used this story as an anecdote during his many talk-bits.

My parents lived under adverse conditions and dire poorness. The single rectangular sod-abode had to do for a few years before the shanty-kitchen was built on. The floor of the sleeping room was partially boarded, merely a frame around the cellar-door to hold for contact. The bare earth-spots were covered with gunney covering.

The cellar slanted inwardly to prevent caving, allowing a lesser spot for setting perishable foods to be kept chilled. What memories of that cellar! It was Dilda's chore to set down a pitcher of milk, but one time she darted up the wooden rungs of the ladder and shrieked ... I so much wanted to go down and see what was there. I didn't apprehend the gist. Dadee stilled the frightful cry and went down himself with a durable stick and scoop as Momee held a lighted match into the dark, so for Dadee to see better. In short order, after a few grunts and wacks, the reptile was slain and shoved onto the scoop and covered with loose dirt. Ye guileless child! So much for undue interest. The lizard could have been a novelty!

The bedroom surface was leveled earth, smeared smoothly with a gumbo-goo and left to dry. Innocently I tracked into the fresh smear leaving footprints. "Du lousz, über alles kommscht nah!" (You louse, into everything you get!), uttered Momee. She was by nature a meticulous woman. Any muddling for disorder Momee would shake her head and the gold earrings would jingle, which added a glitter as she talked. Her up-combed hair, twisted into a bun, indicaterd distinction as an attractive woman with a longing for nicer things. The gold earrings were her last dowry gift from her father.

Momee was raised at Russia's time of better economic thrive and came from one of the most prosperous colonies, 'Groszliebental' of South Russia. The Steinert family were considered well-off. Christina was reared in a well-kept, six-room German colonist-house. She received a good dowry, but the Russian 'rubels' were used up pretty much for the migrational expenses to America. Then to add to the Neher destitution, the Russo-Japanese War soldier-husband received no government compensation ... neither did he receive financial aid from the poor Neher elders. The settling to this wild prairieland life, with poverty at every end, played a gradual havoc on Momee's constitution. And with the room congested with children and two adults, she would relent to irritability.

Very few female children during this era received approval for schooling. Their status was generally deemed lower than that of a male-child. Especially in the field of peasantry, a girl's maturity strongly indicated bearing children, raising and teaching them the work-tasks, whether for the household needs or for oxen labor in the field. The parents of a grown son generally picked the bride for him. It was essential that the daughter-in-law be a speciman of a maiden with a strong back, and that she know how to take the raw elements to be able to make them palatable to eats and dress.

Christina Neher represented a host of young wives who lacked the innate talents of fitting into the prairieland's forceful expectations. There wasn't enough know-how, especially to meet with the demands of a wilderness life. Yet, through the eyes of a child I saw Momee as pretty. The dangle of the gold earrings added to her attractiveness. In moments of repose I would look at her as she sat on a chair.

I developed a love for the outdoors. Vividly I recall Momee cooking and baking outdoors on a sort of open grate of a stone-lined fireplace. I see her turning a loaf of bread on the primitive kiln, having had a hard time keeping the loaves burning to a crow-black on one side, and on the other side it remained a whitish appearance, hardly baking. She got agitated: "Ach Gott, was noch alz!" (Oh God, what else yet!) This was a common outcry. To have good bread demanded too much of her will, invariably causing an upset. I scampered about the place and found the twirling smoke and scorched bread rather exciting. A child's fancy.

I was small in height. Very likely easier to overlook. Probably assumed I still lacked strength for work. Though clever, ready to sneak away as circumstances got frenzied. When once outdoors Momee could not catch me. I could run fast at most any direction to prevent from being seen. I wanted to be in my own world. It could be I'd hide behind a massive stone or lie flat down nigh a sagebrush with its grayish-green branch lapping over me. Momee had a concern as to where I was. When Beller was yet alive I was easier detected since he rallied and sniffed around the hide-out. I never chose to be found for paddling would have been in order.

At about this time I had hunger-pangs. The prairie-rose-hip, still in its tender green form, was some nurture. The hillside gave a place to the wild-rose and throughout the season it offered happy taste to the prairie-child. First, the sweet-tasting petals, then the tender pod, and after Jack Frost's visit, the rose-hip. It can well be called Prairieland's sweet and good communion ... a kind of eats for roamers. Nature saying, "Eat of it ... it is soul-food!"

I scampered down to a low-land to grasp the full-grown grain-heads of which Beller and I used to feed on. The aroma of dumplings was in the air because Momee fried them outdoors on the grate. I heard Dilda calling. Reluctantly I strolled homeward and found everybody around the table ... Dadee at the head. The little girls were seated behind a long-boarded table which was nailed onto two sawed-off tree trunks. The bench likewise was made of a roughly-cut board. Nothing wrong except for the slivers that penetrated occasionally into someone's posterior. It hurt when touched so Dadee pulled the nuisance out after the bloomers were pulled down. In the case of a rather wide splinter, as was stuck deep in a sister's seat, Dadee pulled it out with a plier ... Oh, how she cried! Momee dabbed it with warm camomile tea and consoled: "Sei ruhig, des hailt wieder." (Be still, this will heal again.)

The family members sat around the table and as of mutual habit, folding hands in unison for prayer: "Komm Herr Jesu sei unser gast; Der seine gnade über unz laast!" (Come Lord Jesus be Thou our guest; let Thine grace to us be blest!) The little ones prayed one by one, "Abba lieva Vater Amen." (Abba, dear Father Amen.)

The pan-full of dumplings disappeared all too fast. A one-rabbit stew meant a fragment of meat for each hungry mouth. Momee realized we were still hungry. She broke bread pieces into a bowl-plate, sprinkled on sugar and poured milk over it. This babyish food became a kind of a style for my eats. For the food in the bowl was practically gone when it got to where I sat. It was never enough, not for my sisters either, but I always thought I got the lesser.

Following the milk-pap I was given a piece of heel-bread for to chew and suck on as I drooped down for a nap. For Momee it was important that her children take noon naps, however as I grew older I couldn't abide with her command. There was too much to go for. Even in the confines of the doze-nook my eyes were enlivened by the small details.

On the gumbo-smeared floor I saw a few ants scurrying about, and as I crawled to where the swarm was, Momee noticed the peculiar crawlers and promptly swept up the ants. Even the bitsy dirt mound, throwing it outdoors into thin air. Dismayed I whimpered a bit but soon became aware that a number of busy-bodies were spared the shove. I placed a speck of bread thereabouts and soon the crumb was covered with ants. As though the instinctive call gave the clue for a social feed. Such it was. The crumb began to move ... three motion-filled ants pushed and pulled the particle of bread toward the outdoors. Was it to be a social colony moved away from the danger point? Bound to be.

It seemed my trust in the outside world was inborn. Whether it was an animal, a bird, reptile or insect, I felt perfectly comfortable and at ease in its presence. Oh, for the living habitat on the open prairie! Here is for a passion ... a strong amorous feeling – a trust!

So naively I felt safe until Momee's screams and prompt paddlings roused a feeling of impending danger. Much had to be learned, often by way of a close call for life. As when the irate animal claimed its ground and charged forcibly. Like a bull, a rattlesnake or a vicious dog. I could easily have been the victim of irrational animals.

I had a distinct fascination to pull a dog's shaggy tail, or hold a cow's appendage during the cow-chow.

Then I would dare an act of braiding the long ends of the tail. Likely an unexpected pull spurned the cow to kick, throwing me to a shocking heap. Yet I didn't heed.

I practiced the cunning trick of hanging on to a calf's tail. As the frightened calf scampered over the hill I floundered along holding on to its tail as likened to a rodeo act. I received direct reprove from Dadee as he cracked the whip at a different angle to terrify both calf and provoker to a disentangle. As quickly as the tail-lurch began it subsided.

"Schaedel" was a bull-calf and he grew fast through my hovering over him. He was pail-trained and got more than his share of milk. Tame and yet bold. He got quite daring one day and ventured into the door of the shanty-kitchen where he caused bungling, sticking his head into the slop-pail and over-turning the works with Momee frantically trying to push out the hoodlum. Schaedel went stir-crazy circling the kitchen finally bursting through the door and over a wooden stand, sending it flying into fragments. Momee was weeping in fright. Shortly following this uproar Dadee put a halter on the outlaw and guided him along the side of a horse, which he rode to the Matt Crowley ranch and exchanged Schaedel for a female calf. This created another 'homesick' trauma in my childhood life. After all, Schaedel didn't mean to hurt anyone. To me he was a thriller!

The shortage of all-around items which were needed for everyday use was prevalent during Homestead times. Not likely that each child in the family could claim a cup of her own at meal-time. Elza and I shared the same cup. She had the habit of holding fast to the metal cup which contained milk. Elza drank with loud gulps. She dipped chunks of bread into the milk and drooled as she ate it. As I pouted I watched Elza and waited for my turn. I see four-year-old Elza slouched down in a corner next to the kitchen stove emoting a kind of low-groan before falling asleep in a half-keeled-over position. She developed the habit of sucking her thumb after the bread-node diminished. She appeared to be a picture of a forsaken child.

At last it was my turn for the cup. What a useful thing this dish could be for me! I could fill it with grain or grass heads, or to fill it with pebbles; or, for to dip out water from the dam/brook, to quench thirst, or to catch a squirm. However, the trouble was Momee kept eye's watch on any stunt of hiding the dish for to take outdoors. To own a cup would have been a child's desirous possession.

Barefoot time began as early as a child could walk. Summertime meant that kids were to harden the soles of their feet. For health reasons as well as saving on shoes. As a child I could run lightly over and into any prairie-range with swiftness, barefooted. The bottom surfaces of my feet matched the paws of a dog or cat. Quite tough. However, cactus stickers had a way of penetrating into the tender sides of my foot. Sure. I pulled it out myself except when the burr would break leaving a particle in the flesh to fester. And hurt. Then Momee would bind on a pasty onion-smear with a rag tied around it. An overnight nuisance. It must have drawn it out for I wasn't laid up, not to my recall. To be making a salve from herbs and onions was as much a practice as making a food-dish from scratch. Many a pioneer country kid never got to see a doctor least of all being treated by him. The area midwife served as a doctor as well as delivered babies. However, mostly home remedies consisting of 'smear and sweat' was the general practice for every kind of ailment. Along with 'brauching' (spiritual balm).

Prairieland's roads meandered around and over hills and through vales. There was one straight-way road running from east to west, a mere bit north of our homestead yard. We could not detect any kind of a driver in a horse-hitched vehicle until his sudden appearance. A hill hid the view.

One hot summer's afternoon something like a phenomenal black cart-like huckster wagon with two black horses hitched onto and two mysterious-looking men seated high up suddenly drove into the yard. I ran into the house to tell Momee. At first she seemed overtaken with fear ... then with a sudden burst of confidence Momee walked with a determined pace up to the vehicle and ordered the gypsies to leave. The men chattered eerie talk and directed the team over to the chicken coup. Momee signaled 'der hund'. The dog growled and nipped a horse's fetlock. The mare snorted and ascended into a charge ... then off to a a galloping pace the team raced westward leaving a burst of a dust-cloud as the remnant. Although excited Momee laughed out loud as if to accredit herself for her bravery: "Die zugeiner, die griegen net unzere hehner." (Those gypsies will not get our chickens.) She petted 'der hund' who really dogged them away. He was Momee's sovereign watch dog and for a matter of due 'der hund' lapped up milk-soaked bread, then sniffed agreeably at Momee.

Saturday evening baths! A wash-tub with a bit of heated water gave way to swirling steam. It sat in the middle of the kitchen. Then one kid after another had to get undressed and lunged into the tub as Momee washed and soaped down the naked body with homemade lye soap. She would add a dipperful of hot water after each exit. A part of an old edge-frayed bed-blanket served as a towel for the whole lot. Each one stood ready for a nightgown or a pair of underwear, then shooed off to bed.

It seemed I got the last bath everytime for too often I wasn't at hand. I hated to slouch into the offensive kind of slimy water. I had developed a kind of a shyness about my naked body. To be seen was like I saw my sisters ... any naked exposure was bound to be shamed.

One particular Saturday evening bathing time was somewhat different. Momee placed the tub outdoors after a hot day. My intuitive eyes were focused on the dam just a bit westward and down the hill. I lurked away quietly, undressed and slid yieldingly into a blot of water that contained wriggling movement; then in a comfortable sitting position I cupped with hand the squirmies applying mind to study these wrigglers. Then at a most inappropriate time Dadee comes down the hill. I sense punishment. With a sudden burst I headed farther into the dam. An abrupt fright and a quick slide I sank to the dam's depth. Dadee rescued this rebel but not without a good number of resounding spanks on my bare rear. It was to be understood that there are some things around the prairieland that are to be heeded and feared. And paddling sense into children was the accepted training school. All in all my trust in a large body of water lessened as well as the feeling of security among humans.

A Sunday was hailed. Neighbors would bring their families and gather at one or the other of the sod-house homes. An extra bench was tossed into the wagon and then shoved into the largest room. At our homestead dwelling, worship services were held in the kitchen. Adults sat on chairs and bench and children on the floor. I clearly see Dadee handing out "Evangelium lieder bucher" (Evangelical song books) on a share-basis. Usually a man would start singing the hymn and direct the tune to the beat of a foot and all would join in with hearty voice and sing "Grosser Gott Wir Loben Dich" (Great God, We Praise Thee). Scripture reading from the family Bible followed. In German, of course! The leader was a man who could read and who was right with the Lord. He would explain, gesturing with hands in order to get the message across. Then all "bekehrten" (converted) would fall on their knees and pray orally. Some of it got pretty loud.

Mothers tended to be in the background in an "untertan" (subject) position. Most of them could not read and after all, the Apostle Paul clearly stated that woman be beneath man, the sovereign. In any wrong move man scolded her.

I slipped into the bedroom and I saw mothers breast-feeding their babies. I watched one mother in particular. She unbottoned the front of her dress, swished out one pliant, milk-filled breast, grasped the brownish nipple and pressed it into the crying baby's mouth. Then the tike's cry turned to a desirous draw. This impressionable breast-view of nursing mothers had baffled me to all ends. You see, to expose any bare part of a body called for disgrace ... indecency. Even from small on little girls were told to cover every part of her body, and here I stand and see it all on a woman ... "Ach", what innocence!

This same breast-viewed mother left me with a perceptive picture. Her hair hung in strands, loosened from the bun which hair pins did not hold together. The likely fact she had no time to comb the hair. She looked rather distressed. She prayed out loud as she nursed the baby, displaying an innermost need. Naively I watched her. Later on I surmised this: There was a common homesickness for the "dorf" (colony) life in New Russia where these girls that are now wives grew up. There they tended to be more in company with each other, where they could express their wishful thinking. A wife, to be the subject to her husband often proved a miserable experience, married to a man she hardly knew. However, occasionally one upright pillar of a woman stood out and directly demanded her human dignity so to be more than to be treated as an ox. Here was borne a hint of America's freedom for human respect! However, yet long off for such consideration.

On the whole life was tough on the man too. He held responsibility to feed the family. He lacked knowledge and the means to bring the wilderness to produce. Food was scarce. Naturally malnutrition. That caused irritability. And everything had to be done by the sweat of a man's brow. Man had to devise a way through hit and miss. At best when man and woman jointly worked on circumstances together. "Man-the-ruler trend yet sustained. Be it reasonable or unreasonable! Her call to God for justice strengthened. The man-made law had its stay ... the sufferable innocence, though the way!"

I picture a scene of animation in the 'homestead' yard. A mother-duck and three nearly full-grown ducklings strut through the yard toward the dam. Any tamer they could not have been. I walked by pomp alongside. I talked familiar words and mother-duck quacked in response. You see, we were cronies.

Near a large protruding stone on the east leaning of the yard a female duck formed a snug nest early in the Spring and laid an egg into it every couple of days. I had found a stone that resembled a duck egg. Dadee indicated that I place it into the nest, then carry the real egg to the house for safe-keeping from Spring's frost. Momee carefully placed the egg in a cloth-lined box and shoved it under the bed. After six eggs accumulated, the duck moodily sat on the disguise. Momee placed the real eggs in the nest and removed the stone. Mother-duck resisted with a flap of wings and a hiss, snapping at Momee. With a bystander's help we managed the exchange. Soon mother-duck tenderly pushed, with her bill and wings, every egg under her warm depressed body, resting fixedly. I received stern orders to stay my distance. How could I? The broody-duck relied on water-soaked bread and a handful of grain to feed on.

In due time four ducklings hatched. This was a time when Momee and I together caressed the hatch. Momee appeared exhilarated. Could it be that she saw a worth in this one stone? One weakly duckling died. Momee would not allow "der hund" to have it for feed. It would invite a dog-appetite for ducklings. The three healthy ducklings grew fast. Mother-duck quacked protective orders as she led her brood through the yard down to the dam where water's life was duck's environment. They were not to be hurried. What a sight for a lesson that "hurry is futile". As I ponder on the very stone that sheltered the ducklings, I sense a halloo. This stone could tell the story and boast of its worth, as a refuge to a nest that gave life to the 'homestead' yard.

The 'homestead' yard domesticated another family of web-footed fowl ... a small flock of geese that too found the marshy dam its retreat. This late summer evening the flock was driven into a shelter so Momee could pick the downy-feathers one more time. Early next morning Dadee snatched Mr. Gander with a wire-hook. It took two adults to battle the hostile encounter into a position where Momee could pluck the finery of Gander's feathers. It was not a man's work but the male of the goose required the man of the 'homestead' to handle him. Dadee carried the feudal gander a ways down the hill before releasing him. I ran alongside and noticed the angry fowl stiffen, then thud into Dadee for rebellion. Dadee laughed as though he was proud to have been the conquerer.

Dilda and Odeela helped Momee catch one goose at a time. To position the fowl between the picker's knees and to select only the finer feathers had to be a skill. Even at a better pluck the goose would twinge. Momee seemed pleased as she tossed each jot of feathers into a wash-tub. What gain for a downy pillow!

The next morning I visited for inspection the half-naked flock of geese. Virtuously I drew too near the gwa-auck, gwa-auckers. The gander made a direct dive at me flapping his sturdy wings in a mean slap. Then he pricked my bare legs ... a fierce beak-bite it was! Naturally the angry gander retaliated from yesterday's plight and to take protective measures for his flock. No gander ever makes amends! Herewith I never trusted a gander again.

I was a frightened and hurting little girl as the open sore bled. I ran, aiming toward the direction where Mutter Boehler lived. The vigilant woman fetched the loose-running child and groaned: "Ach du kind, du haasht a-a weh!" (Oh you child, you have a sore.) She daubed the wound with her kind of herb-salve. Distinctly I remember Mutter Boehler as a kind of a Mother Hubbard. As she pushed a chair to the same spot in our kitchen, she would sit there and await for me to crawl on her lap. She held on to me with one hand and with the other gestured for effect as she talked. Her breath seemed sour. I felt a soothing for my inner needs on her soft lap. She truly exemplified a prairieland "mutter" (mother).

During 'homestead' times for neighbors to communicate, mainly messages were delivered by foot or by way of horseback. The onrush of a bareback rider that came galloping along the summit of a long-stretched hill meant a sign for help. Accidents, sickness or plain loneliness. Innocently neighbors searched for answers to problems and relied on each other's advice or help. Or, by way of oral calls, to God Above.

Again, the hilltop was chosen. Generally the mother trudged wearily to the top of a nearby hill and with outstretched hands loudly called on God. Could it have been she chose the hilltop to be closer to the rainbow where the promises were and where "Der Heiland" (the Lord) without doubt was alive and He heard? She asked for their needs to be met and that there be better days ahead. Coming down the hill she walked with surety. Her steps were light. Her faith serene and her trust assured. Anyway, there was strength for the day!

The Bible in most homesteads was the single reading material and in many families only the man could read. News passed mostly by way of hearsay without confirmation. Dadee had an innate interest in world affairs, especially in politics. He loved to make his way to Matt Crowley for reasons other than to bewail for want. He saw an English newspaper and signaled to Matt for explanation when the word Russia stood out in bold print. Matt teased that Ludwig had to learn the better language, the English, in order to get the news. "Ja, ja," Ludwig admitted. The realization took its first note. He sensed the necessity but to keep the family intact in the German language has got to be retained. The German language must eventually rule. So thought Neher as well as all other German-background settlers. The language barrier reached confusion. The stubborn German in no way yet would relent to English.

Children were raised to work. For children to play discerned naught. It would hinder their worth for life. There was the fear of them growing up to a good-for-nothing. The necessity for children to play was never known to be important. Too much expediency and sense for responsibility was expected of children. The knowledge of child psychology too often lacked reasoning ... even compassion. "Spare the rod and spoil the child" ... a much too stern motto adhered to. Discipline matched the training to act much in the manner of force as the practices of medievalism. A lack of humaneness. Oh, for the mixing in of rudeness into innocence!

Compared to my sisters I was littler in size, therefore they befitted better to work while I had the advantage of being footloose. Dilda and Odeela were tending to pieces of work while I was running about the hills. Mutter Boehler fetched me back to the home and to keep company with Momee as well. I liked that. I dared wherever this woman sat to crawl on her lap so to listen and watch. I see Momee hold Louiza. As the child laid across her lap, Momee took a spoonful of "kindes brei" (sauce-like gruel cooked up with flour and milk) and put the substance into her mouth, swished it around so to mix it with her saliva, then ejected the stuff on the spoon and fed the child. This was the standard baby food and strongly advocated by mid-wives. I loathed that sight to a point of heaving. The sauce that was left Momee tried to feed to me in a similar process. I rebelled as any little rebel could ... even tightened my closed mouth. Mutter Boehler urged: "las sie geh" (let her go). Even though her breath smelled too, that my sensitivity tolerated. What a day for emotional incidents that held innocence yet forthright insight!

Even as a child I suffered repugnance for offensive smells. People labored arduously which resulted in free perspiration that emitted offensive smell. Then too clothes absorbed barn-smell and with only one change of garb a week, the odor inclined to that of stink.

So much family had to crowd into one room for night sleep and the nearly steady use of the night-pot left an overall fetidity which made my sensitive nature repugn. I would sneak outdoors early in the morning and do my necessary discharge a little ways from the house where I could grasp a cluster of grass for wiping. Rarely did I settle in the back-house ... not in the summer time. I guess I wanted to imitate the kin-animals and nothing was more soothing as "der hund" sliding close by me as I sat in a bent-posture pose. If the cows could dump on the prairies then so could I. We had stern orders not to do our toilet-duties inside any barn nor behind any abode. An order for cleanliness ruled in our family.

I had an inborn interest in the yard animals. Our parents were less than candid about animal mating habits. When rooster crowed the morning wake, I dawdled around and watched the hen/rooster demonstrative meet; or, during the duration of animal heat in the acts of the male animals we were shooed away. No one told us children what we wanted to know ... eventually the issue of innocence turned to quest. I chased after prairieland's creatures, observing their sensual natures. I basked in the many little animal dramas. Those were moments of learning all by myself. Remembered also are brief instances of fright. As when Momee asked me to gather the dry cow-dabbles along the hill's pasture so to use for stove fire to cook supper on. Unexpectedly the bull of our small herd of cows charged and I slid behind a large stone. What a timely maneuver!

There are strange incidents flashing out of my conscience during the 'homestead' times of my life. I was given a bucket for to help carry water from the dam into the boiler which set on the cast-iron stove. Momee carried two pails. I ran ahead of her and stepped into the cove of the dam where the water was clear. Above the sky I heard the "kill-dee" cries of a few ring plover-birds swooping down for a warning on a probable too-close invasion to their region. The outcries were not the wailing kind ... moreso a happy appeal it sounded like. I wanted to mimic for happiness, but Momee disrupted. The duty to dip clear water into the pails she summoned. I would have rather remained in company with heaven's birds than lugging water for wash-day. Momee was a ways ahead. I noticed a minute froggie, very tiny, squirming about in my bucket of water. I settled comfortably on a stone behind the chicken coop. Then, with dipping action of my hand, I played and talked with a new little pet. Momee appeared and as usual in a hurry ... snatched the pail and before a child's crushed spirits, froggie and water were poured into the boiler. The job of washing clothes had to be done.

How I remember that wash-day! Momee swished back and forth Dadee's soiled overalls on the long-planked table with prolonged and short strokes ... water sipping through without Momee knowing it. The innocent obviousness on the watch for the froggie not realizing that the hot water destroyed it. Momee did not know how it hurt me.

Dilda and Odeela carried the dark wash to a closeby yard-fence and hung it there. The barb-wire took the place of clothes pins and depending on the strong wind Momee's mending and patching work increased. A large piece of wash generally was draped over stone or bush. Momee did not have the convenience of a wash-line nor clothes pins ... not yet.

The shanty kitchen had been attached to the rectangular sod-made abode in about 1912. In the following years the kitchen had taken on a furnished look. I see a self-made long table with a plank-made bench nailed against the wall. Here is where the girlies slid in when it was eating time. The bowl-like dishes had cracks and chip-blots and each of us knew which belonged to whom, often engaging in dispute. "Sen Schtill!" (Be quiet!) was the command. Then we would settle down, fold hands and pray the common child's prayer: "Abba, Lieva, Vater, Amen!" (Hail Dear Father Amen). Each of us prayed separately.

After breakfast Dadee would fetch the large German Bible from a higher-up shelf and read and pray which didn't make sense to me. But we learned to be attentive. On another shelf stood the kerosene lamp and a box of matches as well as a round can of carbolic salve which Dadee used for boils. The shiny drug-store can appealed to me ... what a plaything it could be!

The shanty was a busy place. I see Momee shaking a gallon-pail that contained cream --- whish-whoosh-whoosh! It seemed like an endless job until the cream turned to butter. But tonight she didn't mind. It was one of those rare times Momee received personal regard from Dadee. He was reading Psalms just to her. You see Momee could not read and as it should be, the man had to convey the Holy Word to her.

The kerosene light flickered throwing dim rays of light over the shanty. Finally the shakes of the cream turned to a clear whish, whish, whish! The cream had separated to butter and butter-milk. As Momee opened the lid, she smiled slightly and was pleased as she took out a yellow cluster of butter which she swirled about in several changes of water, then formed it into an oblong mold. The buttermilk, after it had been cooled in the cellar, disappeared all too fast. A glass of buttermilk along with "schtroodle" (strudel), or we drank it for lunch. The way Momee churned butter and Dadee reached for the Bible became a sacred ritual between the pioneer man and woman. A kindly gesture mixed with the divine. I sat on a box and observed an evening hour of shanty contentment. Momee appeared in quiet submission with a smile on her face.

The sod-abode by now was primarily used for sleep. Even though a family of seven crowded the room. It held two beds with straw-mattresses, goose-down pillows and patchwork covers. Between the beds stood a five-gallon pail, topped by a wooden cover with a kind of a tear-shaped hole. This was the night toilet. Every morning it was carried out and emptied into a trench. Dilda and Odeela were carriers. It wasn't a pleasant chore. The sisters were of even height for a balance, but their tempers reckoned an imbalance. Again I was lucky to be the small one.

The two south window-inlets, where sun's rays gradually moved across the room, proved to be the pleasant spot. Through it I could see the hill to the south where I yearned to chase the calves. I'd crawl into the one inlet and do a child's dreaming. Although my reveries were usually outwitted. I dared not crawl into the next insert for Momee had several plants setting there ... geraniums and one "peterling" (parsley plant). Parsley sprigs made the noodle soup something special for Sundays. I was warned not to finger around the plants, but who could resist when a geranium bud burst into a fiery red bloom. What color! For color lacked in those days. Every man-made thing, the making of goods and ware was manufactured in drab colors. Except what Mother Nature produced in her seasonal colors that eventually manifested a color-blush into life!

All dwellings on the Neher homestead were scurried into place. It had to be done in a hurry and made up of prairieland's substances. Sod-barns raised from dugouts were divided into stalls to house the little stock that Ludwig Neher accumulated those first years. A hog-and-chicken shelter had been erected west of the house, whereas the stock shelter was located a bit to the southeast and the hand-dug, stone-lined well inclined to the south of the 'homestead' yard.

The walls of the rude shelters were mainly made with flat-clay mortar and prairie stones. To exist under the rigors of Winter's cold the pioneers labored arduously and with great difficulties during the Summer and early Fall seasons to have it ready when Winter set in. Both man and woman used their physical energy to the limit. For survival reasons. Of report in one homestead the only milk cow was brought into the sod-house to keep udder's teats from freezing. Too many settlers did not anticipate the fierceness of Plains States' winters. Often drastic suffering resulted, as with not enough fuel, food and feed. Setting traps to catch a rabbit for stew for a family of hungry mouths and digging at a coal vein under snow was not uncommon.

Cows got bred at random and calves appeared at critical-time drop. Dadee would bring a newly born calf into the kitchen and lower it onto a gunney-sack in front of the stove. I see it struggling to rise on its own feet and blindly pushing its way hither and thither, spilling the water-pail and searching for its instinctive suck. I tried to take a hold of the calf but its slippery hide stopped that. It was havoc, but I liked the excitement. Dadee milked the kicker-cow for the first slimy-milk which had to be injected into the calf's stomach as its first food and the vital nutrition.

Bossie, the gentle milk cow, could have been called the 'homestead cow'. She was given to Dadee by Matt Crowley as a young heifer sustaining to near calving which was out of season. It would have been a hindrance to Crowley's cow herd. Therefore Crowley tended again his mercy to the desolate homesteader. Neher could break the youngling into a milk cow so to have milk for himself and his family through the direst summer months of 1910.

Bossie had been trained as a young cow to come into the yard and stand by a familiar stone waiting to be milked. The summer's afternoon milking act remained a practice for many-a-moon. Bossie was getting to be an older cow who had endured that of prairieland's harsh realities. The rigors of fiercely cold winters and summer's heat, along with worm infestation and fly plague, weathered the good old stand-by cow to a state of slow, deliberate moves. It seemed the 'old faithful' reveled in the luxury of a stroking. She wanted to be treated special, it seemed. Easily understood, she deserved caressing.

A well-worn tin cup and metallic pail matched the looks of the cow, tainted for a story of hardship's goodness; the mooing of the cow until the milker comfortably sat on a stump-stool and began to pull the plump teats squirting the milk into the pail. Then Dadee would dip with the tin cup into the frothy cow-warm milk, drink to his stomach's content, then fetch out a cupful and hand it to me. No milk ever tasted better. I drank it fast for I wanted a second cupful. I had my eyes on the empty cup ... how I longed to claim it so I could fill it with the variety of pebbles that I gathered as I searched the gumbo patches. I never did get it. The cup/pail ensemble and Bossie cow remained the fixed characters on the west edge of the 'homestead' yard.

The slanting length of hills, all around the homestead, regarded as a more rock-strewn country, contained stones and stones of a variety of sizes. Never was there a good word said about stones by any settler. Rocks over the prairieland were a bane since no standard piece of ground could be plowed without the hindrance of them. Here is where the stone-boat became a vital device as well as a loathe to the kids. To pick up stones from plowed fields and then heap them on the horse-hitched stone-boat, leading the horse to an outer stone-pile and again unloading one by one had gotten to be a hateful job. I was old enough to lead tame Bay to and from stone to pile while Dilda and Odeela carried on and threw off stone after stone. They were only children and their labor agony shed a kind of an impression which I remembered as that of torture. A fonder use of the stone-boat rallied as we filled a barrel with water which we dipped from a clear pond and had Bay pull it home. Naturally there was spill as the stone-boat leant according to the bumpy pasture. I liked the excitement of the splash. And to go back for a refill meant more play-time with the pond's squirmies. Momee needed the soft water to wash clothes. For her time was pertinent; as to me, time was "what's next?" for more exciting venture.

The north side of the sod-house had no windows. I often sat there on the bare ground and studied the north hill where the familiar stones harbored small animal life: the gopher that stood up on its hind legs and shrieked a protective note as it darted into a hole; an occasional rabbit following its trail, wary of a hunt; and birds of a flock trusting its nest near a sagebrush. For no particular reason I slumped over in a laying-down position as any tired little girl would. I had no blanket or pillow. The ground roughness was alright for I'd twist my head and body into a stillness as my eyes were focused to the heavens above. I watched the fleeting clouds. It was like snow-patches moving ... suddenly the shape of a running rabbit appeared. Could it be the same one that lingered about the hill? Then a fleecy lamb rollicked in a frolicsome manner. Another cloud loped and moved in a leisurely way shaping into a man's face. I could envision a chariot. How I desired to sit in this imaginary pleasure carriage. I could ride by the close drifting cloud and touch the beloved fleecy lamb and race ahead of the jumpy rabbit and shout an acclaim for winning the race. As my eyes closed to a sleep, the dream affirmed the fantasies which truly were real, so relevant and so natural. It was prairieland's angel that provided, during my growing-up years, a linkage to Nature's creatures as though we were essential beings to each other.

After the repose I would tread up the hill where the reflective animals of the clouds were real but at this hour of the day larger animals were not around. The smaller stones took my attention. I lifted one and found a number of skirmish ants and larvae. Under another stone an earthworm with a longated body, moving and creeping, trying to burrow into the earth. It was something about turning over smaller stones, one found the smaller creatures in fewer numbers ... thus a single observation. In all innocence I felt a closeness to all life under a stone. I would chatter with them. Except once, I rolled a larger stone and saw a snake suddenly twist into a ring with its fanged head stuck up, sticking out its tongue and making a hissing sound. I had had another snake encounter near the sod-house and since then I dreaded particularly the snake's open fangy-mouth and its cold, slimy form. Here is where Nature failed to give such reptiles a body-of-warmth. The open tongue-lash mouth with its hiss to strike instilled a horror. I could never talk to a snake. Simply to run away in fright. I realized I could never be a crony to a reptile.

Dadee was great at talk, shifting from a tempermental version to a laugh-story. He repeated, telling the plight of their first year on the homestead: "I would sit on a stone and wipe the sweat from my face and think of my mother as I shouted out loud, 'Mutter, you wanted your son to have land ... I've got it now but I must have gotten what the Devil handed out; to spade-dig the clayish earth for a well no task was more excruciating.' I would bend low and cry, then reaching to pick up the jar of clabber stuff of sour milk, damned to drink it for energy. I hated the stuff nearly as much as I hated the sauerkraut that I was forced to eat during Russia's war. I would stand up and see the stony hills and end up gazing into East's horizons ... so very, very far away was level land that my mother had longed for and never got. Well, I didn't get what I had hoped for either. 'Oh, dear Mutter,' it's only good you aren't aware of my distress!"

Neighbors shared in the purchase of a scraper. Every dam tells the story of torture for both man and horse. All sod/stone-built dwellings called for back-breaking work. The coal-digging story Dadee related in an acting-out performance, however he readily admitted that coal was something Russia's immigrants did not have. Would it have been better had the Nehers remained in Russia? Mixed thoughts. Tearfully Dadee would change the seriousness of conversation to his own brand of humor, as he wiped and shaped his mustache, he joked that America's coyote taught him more good lessons for survival than Russia's czar ever favored the German colonists with. Of which he was one. As if by common reflection, Dadee would mimic a Russian officer, playing the part of an obvious Bolshevik. What a bewilderment! In one instance Ludwig realized the barren future of his German relatives and friends in Russia; in the next thought he lamented the direful times of taming America's undeveloped prairieland. Here too, an argument for thought ruled. Dadee felt the United States government could have been of some aid. In both countries, the Nehers played the hard part for survival. Either country, it was plight.

Along the side of the tree-cluster hill, a stub of a larger stone clung to the slope and as a child I rallied playfully in hither slides about the slant. I watched the cows drinking by sips and waddling lazily in the dam's border and doing their jobs of secreting as well.
My thirst intensified. I sat down on the edge of the other side of the dam where the water was quite clear. I was rather accomplished in cupping out water with my hollow-formed hand from a brook, pond or stream for drink ... and now, even from the dam. It was good enough for my animal friends, why not for me?
The result of drinking the life-infested water

for Prairieland's children spelled trouble. Unaware of its effects. The life-squirmies in the water which the children drank converted to pin-worms more likely; of the worst kind were tape-worms.

First signs for the ailing children infestation were a lack of appetite and vigor as well as restless sleep. Mutter Boehler knew exactly what was wrong, just by looking at pale faces. Special extraction of juices from certain herbs would do the trick ... then another stronger herb for the tape-worm. At one time all of the Neher girlies were forced to drink the bitter stuff. At Mutter Boehler's reprimand and warning. Oh for the pity of mothers who dealt with worm-infested children! It touched every homestead family at one time or another. How well pioneer children remember the bitter drink and the disembowlment!

Now I am a septuagenarian. I take frequent drives out north to the old homestead place. There are bountiful reminders that stir my memory. Each hill and vale reflects a succession of incidents with vivid impressions, but to hike the trails that wagon and buggy tracked into the prairieland elates and rouses my mental images of the childhood doings. These roads were either dusty with fine, silty soil during the hot summer days or they could become a boggy of mud-mire overnight. I used to sift my bare toes through the silt or the mud which tended to nourish healthy feet. It was equally therapeutic and enjoyable.

The parallel lines of the prairie-road are still evident. Even if the curves near the gulches are overgrown and lined with roots and twigs, the overall road-course is yet visible after seven decades. One particular ant-pile is not there anymore. What a pleasant time I had harassing those busy-bodies. To compensate my evil act, I watched for an opportune time to pour a bit of sugar onto a cloth and form an inconspicuous node ... then hold it in my hand so Momee wouldn't see it, so then to scoot for the ant-mound and sprinkle the sweetness over it. How vitally alive became the ant-hill! A sudden social arousal and in short order two or three ants were seizing and holding fast to one sweet crystal aiming to shove it to safe storage. I carried a branch-stick with me and gently contacted the mound. The ants coated the stick with a substance that had a appetitive taste. It must have been one of Nature's dispel of Vitamin C, a nutritional element supplying the prairie child's craving. I would lick the stick for a tasty smack.

The meandering road, leading west had distinct meaning. It was the road driven most frequently for both happy and sad reasons. It was the road leading to the Martins, the relative-family that had accompanied the Nehers as immigrants from South Russia to America. The two families shared the woes of homesteading. Together they constructed the prairie-abodes, devised ways and means, anguished and argued. Repulsive yet relenting. They needed each other. The Martin family had older children that were helpers ... mainly boys. Neher's family of little girls were yet the sprout for work. Thus the difference in human energy for accomplishment. That made Dadee feel behind and lost. He would beg for help. And Momee would take along the dough, for the Martins had a better-bread-baking stove than the Nehers. It all added up to the key admonition: "You've got to help out!" Despite it all there linked intimate ties and obligations between the Nehers and Martins.

The prairie-road north, over the hill through an extended course of a vale, led to the Bitterman homestead. Here Neher received his first side-pork for sustainable eats as he gazed at 'his land' frightfully, coping with a first step for shelter and swallowing the bit of salt-pork without chewing. No tools and no provisions, not even for a start ... except for a decision to run from neighbor to neighbor and gesture for 'help'! No other 'homesteader' could improvise such a talent!

The direct road east, Neher ordinarily made by foot or on bare horse-back. In review of the first year of homesteading, the Matt Crowley ranch was the main focus. Dadee found it feasible to go by himself. Crowley spoke English, therefore the German families did not mingle in company. Although Neher reasoned for the German language to rule, he found Crowley's English important enough to learn so as to communicate. After all this Irish man seemed better fixed to deal with the raw-elements of the wild-land hardships. Often provoked at Neher's too-frequent visits, Crowley held compassion for the family's dire needs. By way of gesture and word-order, Neher got the message across. Both gained in learning from each other's language, however Neher's deeper motive aimed at begging for the use of Crowley's mower.

The southward road, leading over Neher's table-land, meandered toward the Jaeger homestead; then onward passing through Farmer's Valley where there was a mixture of nationalities of homesteaders, mostly the true Germans.

These horse-drawn wagon trips to Hebron were rare, however exciting. The trips to town left indelible impressions. The slow horse-pace was not tiresome. Dadee's elated. Today the shortage of money didn't seem to bother him. Enroute to town he 'ho'-ed the horses to a halt for rest as he called to the plower of a field for a visit. (Neher was not cut out for farming. He needed to deal with society, not with the wild land.) Parallel trails, rather rutted from the numerous wagons, reached the last hill. Oh, for the creak of the wagon! The team of horses sensed unhitching and blew out their nostrils as the driver saluted the arrival to Hebron.

Other immediate neighbors of the Neher homestead were the Jacob Boehler family, one-half mile northwest from Vater George and Mutter Elizabeth Boehler homestead; the Jack Crowley family lived straight north of the Bitterman place near the bend of the Knife River. To the northeast resided the Burkhardt family, and to the southeast the Fred

Boehler family. Then the two generations of Jaegers lived southeast close to the Neher table-land. John Schnaidt settled on the virgin land one-half mile west of the Martin homestead. Schnaidt homesteaded as a bachelor, then was wooed by matchmaker Ludwig Neher to marry Rosina Winterroth, rather on short timing. Then there were the Opps and Kreins.

The more distant settlers, in all directions, were the Maerschbeckers and the Jacobs families, the Hausauers, the Bauers, the Grumms, the Roeslers, the Schocks, the Lennicks; and the Ochsners and Feils who endured the hilly land for only a short time. The Salmons resided for a number of years a bit north of Matt Crowley where the Mr. and Mrs. served as teachers in the Elm Creek District. Later on the Ed Kreins moved there. What a melting pot!

Ranchers in the wider area of Knife River/Elm Creek country, to my memory-linger, were as follows: Along with the Jack and Matt Crowley ranches were the Backfisch, Keogh, Smith, Hauck, Leutz and Schaeffners. Very likely others. The Walkers were instrumental in opening a frontier-type post-office in the Golden Valley area. Actually, ranching suited this hilly and stony country. Therefore ranchers prospered.

The custom of having parents choose the mate for their grown son or daughter originated in Europe. This practice ruled strongly in the German colonies of Russia ... so that no son or daughter might marry a 'Russ'! It was also vital for a son to marry a girl of good size and strong back, the better to work and be a serf to her man. Marriage-fixing, even if the couple hardly knew each other, tended to be a forced procedure. Many a bride lingered with heavy heart through the wedding ceremony. Women cried, wiping tears on dress hems, in lieu of their own lot for despair and for the pity of the bride who faced life's bargain.

Doubtless to say the traditional practice of couple-matching has tapered off in America. The immigrant settlers' grown sons and daughters resented matchmakers which was a taste for freedom. Not entirely alienated from the custom, parents pointed out to their son or daugher a choice mate, mainly on terms of a dowry and how well the selection of a maiden for the groom merits in the area of being able to work. These had to be stern considerations.

An occasional matchmaker appeared on the scene of a shy loner. As when the lunkhead was tongue-tied and someone outside the family needed to give him a hearty slap behind the shoulder to get him going. And that the damsel is not to be feared, but rather made to feel favored as a first step toward proposal. Then all other details would fall into place. Ludwig Neher served efficiently as a matchmaker. He enjoyed being a matrimonial agent and was proud of an occasional accomplishment. Whether he was ever compensated in pay for his chivalrous favors is doubtful. Rather pleased with his noteworthy act, Neher described the experience with one 'dummer essel' (dumb donkey) with the Bitterman boys and then got boisterous laughter. The Bitterman sons liked this 'Russ' soldier-man who told smart stories. Coming riding on a bare-back horse to where Neher was working, yard or field, posted a common sight. Neher was a spectacle for thought and fun. Very likely the Bitterman boys gathered timely instruction for their nuptial possibilities.

The pioneer son met his girl at a Saturday evening barn dance. Or, he eyed a special one during a church service. As when the older men sat on the right side of the country-church pew and the grown boys a bit farther ahead; then the women and maiden-daughters to the left. Distracted from the sermon, the swain picked out his girl and invited her for a walk during noon hour. He proposed and she agreed. The twain attended the prayer meeting but their thoughts exalted on each other rather than on God. Or, the pair had grown up in school together, herded cattle, played games or roamed the prairies, knowing all along they must tie the knot.

But now where to live? Any place, even if its only in a one-room shack which the squatter left behind. Rather than having the whole shebang under one roof and even if the groom's father governed, but to be alone was likelier for freedom.

America beckoned thousands of young couples to develop the land. What prospect! Neither the meager furnishings nor the simple eats seemed much of a problem. They had intact dreams about 'Open Land'! A challenge for Knife River/Elm Creek country. A specimen of America's prairieland!

The struggle of the Plains' prairielands was one of irregular, tumultuous and unbalanced odds. Not even could the U.S. government provide counsel to the bereft homesteaders, nor were the dire hardships realized. The entire life on the prairies, whether related to animal or man, hung desperately on the notions of the weather. Right temperatures and sunshine could produce a carpet of a green grain field overnight. Russian thistle, rust, insects could spell havoc and hailstorms could pulverize fields and gardens in minutes. However, the prolonged lack of precipitation touched the country with greatest despair. Stock needed a larger range of pasture and fields needed to produce more grain and fodder. Neighbors were far too crowded; the 160-acre homestead demanded expansion and the hoarding of available land spawned rivalry. Cattle broke into the neighbor's field and feuds became bitter. Fencing became a must and one irate neighbor not only damned his neighbor by cursing him, but also warned of his eternal punishment. The two rows of fencing explained the discords.

It had been a rather bleak summer-season. Rain showers were scarce. The fenced-in pasture, southeast of the Neher homestead had been grazed out. Dilda and Odeela were herding the cows a bit to the northeast where the cows could feed . A young leader-cow named Scheck tended to side-track the other cows, leading them to greener pastures. The Burkhardt grain field, near ready for harvesting, was situated on the Burkhardt table flat. Neighbors could not yet afford ample fencing. Scheck's followers infringed upon the field for good chews and the trampled field looked sick. The two little girls were unable to control the head-strong Scheck.

Here resulted a neighbors' feud. It was a bad one. Verbal abuse. Even throwing stones. Neher as well as Burkhardt combined in due proportion of enraged temper. After all, the Burkhardt wheat field was meant for flour to bake bread. "You've taken away the bread from our children!" An excruciating and pitiful scene of pain hovered between the neighbors. The emotional agony on children did greater harm than it did on the elders. The evident hostility had to be faced. The best solution resorted to more fencing or moving elsewhere where there was more land expansion.

Innocently homestead life for the first generation of prairieland children spelled history. Dilda and Odeela were due to attend country school at Elm Creek District 21, School #2. It was late summer (1916) and the barefoot Neher children needed shoes. Dadee loaded up on the wagon some sacks of grain that were to be sold at Hebron's mill. The three oldest of the Neher girls had the privilege of going along to town. One very early August morning Dadee's best team of horses pulled the wagon-load at parallel trail southward. Momee remained home with the two youngest girlies, Elza and Louiza. Her walk was rather slow. Momee was in "andere umschtaenda" (family way).

A mixture of fright and adventure set apart this trip of mine to Hebron. My sisters too were elated, mainly at the prospect of getting new shoes.

Dadee chatted with us as though he felt it a treat to have us with him. After the long but interesting drive to town, the three of us girls were fitted with button-down shoes ... several sizes too large. The shoes didn't impress me as did the variety of things the store contained, the characteristic smell and the various people coming and going. Some talked English like the Crowley man did; others spoke high German; then there was talk like we did at the Neher home, a Swabian German dialect. For a child of hay-seed, it meant for a day of horizon's discovery ... the range of curious things stocking the store.

Enroute home we laid under a cover in the wagon listening to the wagon wheel creaks and the thud of horse hooves that lulled restless sleep. Dadee sat on the elevated wagon seat, jangling the rein-lines and urging the team in his familiar tone 'giddy-up' for a brief trot ... so to make headway to the north. The night wore on and the horses slowed to a walk, seemingly exhausted but sensing home ground. Dadee called the word 'ho!', struck a match and lit a lantern. We three perked up our heads; "Schaffen euch inz haus un gehen schloffa" (get yourselves into the house and get to sleep). Dadee unhitched, watered, fed and unharnessed the sweat-smelling team under the wary light of the lantern. He too was dog-tired, so much that his snoring turned to sounds of snorting.

The goods brought home from town pleased Momee. Some things for food. Her oldest children had shoes and Dilda and Odeela, each a new dress for school. No, Paulie did not get a dress but the lore of town-going engraved a dressier impression than any new dress could have. It was a day to remember!

The Autumn of 1916 showed signs of an early winter. As the older sisters attended school, I spent time in the barn with Dadee. I pulled the cows' tails and braided Bay's tail and pumped water into the trough. The handy pump replaced the pail-pulley-draw. This cold morning the pump apparatus had frozen up. Dadee fetched the tea kettle and poured hot water into the upper part of the pump. Eagerly I went to it, pumping the water as Dadee led the stock to drink. The windy day brought forth the first snowfall. Fred and Margaret Feil and their first child paid us a visit. The Feils likewise took up a homestead among the prairie hills to the southeast. And today they rattled into the yard with a team of grays hitched to the wagon. It was evident these prairieland homestead folks were lonely and sought company. "Haven ihr was zum essa?" (Have you got something to eat?) No issue was made of not knowing of the company arrival. Momee could make something to eat out of practically nothing ... such as 'ein-lauf suppe' (batter soup). As Dadee and I entered the shanty kitchen, Mrs. Feil immediately noticed my very red cheeks: "Child, have you got frost-bitten cheeks?" "No, no," remarked Dadee, "Paulie hat gesunde rote backa!" (Paulie has healthy red cheeks.) Dadee went on to explain that the drinking of cow-warm milk, eating of rose-hips and romping the hills makes Paulie the healthy and red-cheeked child she is. Mrs. Feil related this story in her latter years, recalling the pleasant visit. Without regret the Feils left the homestead shortly enough and moved to Hebron where Fred served as dray-line man.

I remember the tiny heaps of snow along soddy's north wall. Momee stuffed rags into the sod-breaks. In the evening we had to wear long underwear for night-wear ... and after a season of sleeping in nainsook 'hemt' (night-shirt) the discomfort led into irritability as four of us were crowded into the one bed. Wearing itchy underwear led to kin squabbles. I held on with two hands to a gray rag-doll which Mutter Boehler had given to the Neher girlies, the only doll I'd known in the homestead-home. Mutter Boehler had stuffed a gray sock making it look like a funny copy of a baby-doll. Tonight I held it firmly against my chest ... its soothe touched my cheek. It was like 'Cuddles' is to the modern child.

The homestead-doll helped us older girlies to outgrow the suck-node habit. Elza, however, turned from sucking a node to sucking her left thumb. She developed a great fondness for cats and dogs. A scene, where 'der hund' and Elza lay sleeping at close-mode, presented a picture of homestead distinction. Elza's hair matched 'der hund's' belly color — an ash-blond. Animal and child laid on bare ground near the front of the sod-house where sun's rays added warmth. Sleeping in close-clutch and complete repose, Elza, sucking her thumb with one hand and with the other, holding on to 'der hund's' front leg. No akin view could have better described the life of homestead children!

English reading material was scarce, especially among the German-ethnic settlers. At this point there prevailed the stern conception that the German language must suffice and remain the standing and upright language. As the German man had stamina and rightly so his language spelled integrity. No proud German accepted the printed line of an Englishman. English written stuff had little meaning, yet when Neher, a strong German advocate, visited the Crowley ranch, his first reach for something was the English newspaper.

To further hamper the spread of English material, the common saying influenced the whole ethnic-belief: "Papier ist geduldig!" (Paper is patient) meaning, what does the English sheet paper convey? Not much of value.

The German families at this point of time took upon themselves to teach and train their own children in their own culture. Not much emphasis was placed on the literal learning, moreso children were trained for a family-power industry. Some children were kept away from the sprouting country school, therefore illiteracy resulted. The following anecdote described the situation:

The overgrown illiterate son was hired out to a neighbor over the winter for board and room. Johann sat lazily in the corner of the kitchen, dozing and passing time, or whittling on some piece of wood and at the same time befriending the cat. Instinctively the cat made Johann her refuge. The Shep dog too was allowed to come into the kitchen for to lick up the bits of table-food-scraps. Johann threw the cat right on the 'hund's' (dog's) back for a bit of excitement. Shep let out a 'bellen' (bark). Innately a cat will jump or climb the highest point. The cat jumped on Johann's head and clawed firmly on the hired man's bushy, unkempt hair and with her foot-nails clawed the forehead of the poor sucker. The cat-scratch festered. His fate resulted in an onion-plaster tied around the forehead. The remedial treatment, not to allow cold-air contact, kept the jester confined near the bounds of the coal-pail and stove-poker ... his only sensible job to poke out cold ashes and keep the fire going so the woman could cook the 'schtroodle' for his hunger. And 'bitte' (please), woman, make enough so I can feed my closest friend, the 'black cat'! A simile that matched in mental capacity. Everything in stride for survival sake. Even Johann's demands to be waited on, as a male should be, was the good Lord's admonition ... so thought the man! Ignorance in Johann's life definitely was bliss! Johann as well as other young people who were born in Europe and accompanied their immigrant-parents to America, hardly knew what school was like.

Fortunately Knife River/Elm Creek locality of southwest Mercer County were granted English-speaking and school-minded settlers that upheld the need for schools. In 1911 Pauline Shoemaker of Holland Dutch ancestry and a Normal School graduate from Pennsylvania filed on a homestead north of Hebron along the Knife River. Here the neighboring children were pupils in her claim shack for several years. In 1914 she married a neighboring rancher Matt Crowley and moved to the Elm Creek Crowley ranch. In view of their own three daughters Mrs. Crowley asserted with determination for good country schools. And likewise Ruby Crowley, the wife of rancher Jack Crowley, participated in the interests of schools, serving as district clerk for many years. Raising and schooling their eight children, Ruby Crowley contributed substantially in the way of obtaining better qualified teachers for District 21, and Ruby Crowley also nurtured the spiritual needs of the area's many children. She supervised Sunday school in the English language at School #1. She taught the children to sing hymns of praise and reflected a beautiful singing voice. The two Crowley ladies necessitated the English language and made the German-speaking parents realize the importance of America's standard language ... that it be their patriotic duty to accept the nation's language for the sake of their children's future. Obviously America's country schools blended the authentic melting pot into a united educational system that gave the pioneer pupils a start for freedom to rights and opportunity. Finally, the German homesteaders began to accept and gradually relent to the English language.

The crop of babies born at Elm Creek country never depended on Nature's precipitation. A baby appeared in a home without due deliberation. And it wasn't the stork either that brought it, for that prodigious bird remained in Europe. What was seen and believed by the eye witness was Mutter Lennick who added another and another child to the already crowded homes. Rarely was there a family which didn't have between six and twelve or more children.

Mutter Elizabeth Lennick (Mrs. Conrad Lennick) served as the north country midwife for many years. Despite her own family of ten children she never wavered in commitment to take on any confinement case. Occasionally she was assisted by Mutter Carolina Burkhardt (Mrs. Rudolph Burkhardt) who had a large family as well. In crucial delivery cases they would advise each other. A prayer for God's help as well.

The evident drive of the family man as he drove in buggy or sled at horses' trot to fetch Mutter Lennick as quickly as possible seemed to be a natural occurrence. Clad in bulky dark dress-wear, Mutter Lennick's head was wrapped in a black shawl; one hand to keep fast hold on something on the buggy and with the other hand she upheld a bundle in a sizeable garment of a checked apron. For the littler children Mutter Lennick was the mysterious baby-bringer; for the teenagers it was an utterance of: "schon wieder aa baebe!" (again a baby!)

The stork really never inhabited Elm Creek country ... Mutter Lennick brought the babies, snugly wrapped in her apron!

December 21, 1916, was a special day at the Neher homestead: I see Mutter Lennick bring the new baby into the shanty kitchen where all of us girlies had been sleeping on a floor-spread of bedding. She announced: "Ihr hen aa boilee!" (You have a little boy!) A happy note marked our household. Dadee laughed. His exhilaration was contagious

... so much so that the atmosphere created an intimacy of the family. To an extent that the overcrowded home seemed big enough. At last Momee gave the lord-man a son!

The baby was named Edwin, a relatively uncommon name. Usually babies were named for the ethnic-family line. There had to be a Gottlieb, Jacob, Henry, Johann, Friedrich, etc., and in the fair sex, a Mary, Carolina, Eva, Lizabeth, Katherina, etc. When a baby died, then the next one was named after the deceased, a name-sake tradition, especially among the German-background families. Their belief was to honor the spirit of the dead child by passing the name on to the next child.

The German Johannes Gemeinde had been organized in 1915 by a mission minister that represented the German Congregational Church headquarters of the Prairie States. Country churches sprouted over the prairieland. However, the Johannes Gemeinde, composed of Germans from Russia settlers, received permission to use the Elm Creek School #2 to hold their Sunday church services. Evidently Ludwig Neher served as a charter leader. He was the better of intellects ... a natural talent which his dear mother Julianna had endowed him with. As well as taught him to read and write the beloved German language.

The Johannes Sunday School presented its first Christmas Eve program. Dilda, Odeela and Paulie (myself) were taught Christmas "schpruchla" (pieces). Dadee hitched up a team of horses to a sled ready to aim for the schoolhouse. It was a fiercely cold evening and last orders were that Paulie stay home. "Du bischt zu klae-ie ... des isch zu kalt!" (You are too little ... it is too cold). Naturally I threw a tantrum. My cry succeeded. Dadee packed the three of us into the sled with our feet resting on oven-heated stones. Dadee wore the "belz" (overcoat), fleece-lined mittens and cap. Standing in the front, he lightly slapped the reins on the horses' rumps: "Giddy-yap!" And we were on our way as the runners resounded an eery echo suggesting a raw cold. Upon arrival and unhitching at the school yard Dadee threw the robes over the steamy horses and tied them to the sled where they could munch on hay.

The school barn had room for only two teams of horses and as a rule was designated for the farthermost neighbors. All horses needed protection from the frigidness since exposure to severe coldness, after a drive, often caused stiffness which resulted in permanent handicap. This caused friction among Johannes Gemeinde members. Disputes arose. Each neighbor claimed for his rights.

This night Dadee did not argue. The celebration of the gentle Christ Child's birth must have comprehended a solemnness. Or was it the birth of his own son that made him remain collected? Not even did Neher indicate annoyance.

In all ado, I see the full view of a first church-program Christmas tree. It was not an evergreen ... moreso it had the appearance of a bulberry bush tree. The school teacher held over the trimmed tree after having used it for the country school program. Art-paper cut-outs of star and bell emblems added color to the neutral tree and the lit-wax candles of various colors not only livened the tree, it signaled for an easy fire. In all innocence we children couldn't have been less naive about the dangers. The Bitterman family brought with them a can of water to be used as an extinguisher, just in case.

The German Christmas program imparted a spiritual light. Children saw the 'goody-sacks' piled on a heap. Dadee acted as overseer and announcer. He reminded: "Lout un deitlich" (loud and clear). Dadee had admonished his girls to speak the recitations he taught us with strong expression. I walked up the rude platform and faced lots of people who stared at me. My heart fluttered ... so all the more I shouted my piece: "Ich ben a-a klainer wicht; ich kann so fiele saga nicht; doch kommt das Christ-kind herbei; a-a Deutsches Gnad-wort soll Ihm sei!" (I am a little show-off; yet I can't speak much; the Christ Child has come; a German grace-word of Him we touch!) We received our sacks; in it were "nuza, kaendy und a-a bumaronz" (nuts, candy and an orange). To a child, the glitter, to utter aloud my piece and the first bite into an orange ... it couldn't have been better for immediate wants, but the 'best' was the "Gnad-wort" (grace-word) of the Christ Child!

None of the Neher children received actual Christmas gifts except for the candy/nut package. Not up to now. So we knew no better. However, a few days after the Christmas program I accompanied Dadee on another sled-ride, to the Uncle Fred and Aunt Sophie home. Here again the flicker of candle lights animated my whole being. I see the decorated tree setting next to the south wall between two windows in the Martin parlor. Martha, near my-age cousin, untied a red-tissue wrapped bundle, unfolding a white petty-coat with wide lace around the hem. It was Martha's Christmas gift. I stood nearby, longing not so much for the petty-coat, moreso for the rustling red paper ... a child's desire for something colorful! I was too young to realize the lack of money in the Neher home. The Martins all along had a fuller purse. They had more of everything. That was understood since their boys were of expedient age; and Uncle Fred brought with him from Russia some 'rubels' (dollars) which Dadee did not. As a Russo-War soldier, he never got 'rubel'-reimbursed for his military service.

Locally-wise, it has been a rather bleak year ... the crop was not so good. Grain fields produced short-stemmed and partially filled heads. So was the grassland, brief and dusty. Hay and straw denoted insufficiency of quantity. The few cows and horses got thinner as the Winter grew more brutal. The trees in the forked creeks stood bare-branched against the crystal sky. Nature hardly supplied the birds with berries. Feed lacked for prairieland's animals.

Even so, food supplies at our house lessened to the extent that I sensed an overall concern. Momee had stored summer's eggs in an empty nail barrel, layer upon layer, and covered them with oat-grain. Dadee cupped out a half-pail full of oats from the barrel, so to strew a bit over the meager fodder for the stock and for the chickens. To supplement nutriment.

Indeed, even so the food on the family table meant scant helpings. Momee brought the measured milk to a boiling point; then she added hot water from the tea kettle, thus to stretch it. So each child gets at least two-thirds of a cupful. Calves had to be fed ... there too, Momee added warm water. To draw milk from a cow that lacked feed added up to less milk.

Fresh warm cornbread and hot diluted milk was supper. The smaller of the two kerosene lamps flickered its low beam. We used the lamp with the smaller wick that sucks up less kerosene. The five Neher girlies sat around the table, with bowed heads and folded hands praying the German prayer. Dadee sat at the head and Momee portioned out the cornbread and poured the milk. 'Da boylie' (Edwin) was sleeping, not yet aware of the food shortage.

This was a cold, mid-winter evening. As we partook of the simple eats, an abrupt knock and bang hit the kitchen door. As Dadee opened the door, a gust of icy air pervaded the room and was accompanied by a man wearing a sheep-skin coat and fleecy cap with laps. His mustache and beard were matted with ice crystals. What excitement! To behold a 'big-belz'man! Usually when the Bitterman boys paid us a visit there was laughter. But not tonight.

"Our 'Vater' died this day," announced John. "Mutter could not help him anymore; she 'brauched' (meditated) and kept him warm, but Vater struggled to breathe, then took a last breath." The grieved son took Dadee's place at the table and devoured the last piece of corn-meal bread, as Dadee dressed in his 'belz' attire and accompanied John to the Bitterman home.

The dead man Pete was placed inside the granary and placed on a door-frame that balanced on a metal container, so mice couldn't crawl up. He was covered with his favorite quilt and held over for Spring burial. The isolation, lack of communication and rigorous manner of transportation were the reasons for holding over many a dead body for Spring burial during the frontier times.

Often not more than a simple Psalm, meaningfully narrated by a family member or a neighbor, made up the memorial service. The deceased was wrapped in his favorite robe or quilt with an outer cover of gunney-sack, then lovingly lowered into a grave on a spot secluded at random. Frequently the family chose part of the back yard, or a hill-top; or a site where a few others had been buried.

So was the Homestead Cemetery born ... a father and son died in short order from meningitis contracted from the dread horse disease and were buried in a prairieland spot. Here, then, the Johannes Gemeinde purchased a one-acre spot from George and Elizabeth Boehler for five dollars. Here is where Pete Bitterman was buried, George and Elizabeth Boehler as well, and many other 'homestead-times' victims. A guess of over twenty pioneer children and adults are buried here.

It was another Spring, a time for promises and when Nature simply compelled the homesteaders for a new hope. But before the plow was put to furrow, neighbors gathered to pay Pete Bitterman their last tribute. Memorial services were held under the auspices of the Johannes Gemeinde at the schoolhouse. I was at an age when the bond of such happenings held lasting memories. I dared not to attend services but I watched the burial.

The procession of horse hitched vehicles, both wagons and buggies, passed our homestead-home in a sort of a solemn manner. I felt something mystical as wagon and buggy passed by, one by one, the slow moving wheel reeling out an occasional clatter and the bridled horse blowing out his nostril as if sensing unhitching.

With no 'buts' about it, I ran over to where the caravan halted. I discovered an excavation and six men lifting a large box off of the leading wagon, as neighbors gathered around the earthen hole. I felt a kind of a frightful feeling as I sat on a protruding stone, a bit to the east. Momee waved her hand at me, gesturing for me to go home. But I didn't go! I captured the feel of a neighbor man's death and what a big box-bed he had! As it was lowered into the grave, I heard screams of cries. I heard a dignified man dressed in black, step to the head of the earth-hole and solemnly speak: "Es ist Gottes Gnade; staub zu staub." (It is God's will; dust to dust.)

Pete Bitterman charted the Homestead Cemetery ... he who was a pioneer figure of the undeveloped Knife River/Elm Creek prairieland ... he played a part to make a field or two produce for a livelihood. He was often heard to quote: "Wemmer nur essa hen!" (If we only have eats!) Pete Bitterman left his family a legacy --- "a patience for God's prairieland!"

The Farmstead
Prairie's Range

It was early Spring of 1917. The Bitterman boys were reluctant to continue life on the hilly country which their father had homesteaded and gave his life for. After all, a horse-rancher, who had squatted the land adjacent to Bitterman's claim, also died in quick order; and so did his son. Could it be that life among those hills destined doom? It was an omen that brought about changes.

Neher, on the word of trust and honor, purchased the Bitterman homestead and was to be paid off after the season's harvests. The deal was made at the county seat, Stanton, ND. Needless to say, Neher received a winning bargain, for a bare purchase. The Bittermans moved to the Zap, ND, area.

The naive thoughts in my mind, I recall the last days of family life in the congested sod/shanty home. A Spring snow storm was raging outside. I had crawled out of the girl-filled bed much too early because I felt like throwing up. The odors from the hot clinkers adulterated the air. Momee removed the searing mass from the stove with a stove-poker and coal scuttle, in order to make room for a fresh fire. The smell hindered my breathing and caused a burning taste which my stomach could not tolerate. I did heave up the viscid secretion. Funny I found a bare spot to direct the vomit to. Six children and the parents ... eight people sleeping in one room with a mixture of odors; and yet, in my memory there lingered a last close-family repose in the rectangular sod-made room. Where four out of the six children were born in. The room contained family history. Both bad and good. We were the poor of the poorest. Baby after baby, wailing from malnutrition and the wrong treatment-beliefs ... practices that caused a baby pain ... such as binding its navel with a flat strip of white material of several bindings around the poor tike's abdomen ... Oh, so tight! Imagine the discomfort, the pain and distress, especially in the summertime. One of Momee's tender sayings to her whimpering child was: "Kind, geh du schloffa" (Child, go to sleep). Certainly she also needed rest.

Another 'homestead' evening rallies in memory. It was evident that the Neher family would be moving out of the 'hole-of-a-home' shortly. One evening seemed special. Dadee paced back and forth, from kitchen to bedroom, with hands clasped behind his back ... releasing the hands he would scratch his head and wipe a tear. Then, as in somber thought, he reflected. Yes, homesickness touched him. For the moment, did he reflect the benefits this prairie-home had granted them? It had given them survival. It had its "halo"! Four babies were born here and the prayer "Abba, Lieva, Vater" had been taught. Innocence compensated.

Yes, the thoughts of family in Russia entered his talk. Tonight Ludwig would want his dear Mother Juliana to know of the acquisition of much more land. Julianna wanted her sons to have land, whereby they could prosper. Can I have such trust in land as my mother did? Naturally, Dadee pondered.

Momee sat on her favorite chair, close to the wash-basin stand where lay the comb. She unraveled her hair-knot ... a usual bun so formed on every woman's head ... the same style. Tonight she draped her dark hair down and ran the comb through, next she twisted it into a distinctive knot ... then giving the neck-line strands an up-lift stratum as the gold earrings dangled.

Dadee stopped pacing and busied himself, using hands and fingers to demonstrate the hut-home he was raised in as a boy. Momee laughed. She had something over on him. She grew up in the prosperous 'dorf' (colony) of Groszliebenthal. In Russia, as did Dadee. The Steinert home was much more elaborate than the Neher hut. Momee prided herself that she was raised in an "Einheits haus" (unitary house) that combined living quarters for both man and animals; the first unit was the family's living quarter composed of two large rooms, the kitchen and parlor, with two or three smaller rooms diverted for bedrooms. Only families of above-average means could afford such luxury (Christina Steinert was raised in such a home).

Attached to the kitchen wall leant the calf-stall; then the cow shed where the milking-by-hand was done; a roomy stable with numerous stalls for work horses and pony often extended into the back yard; adjacent to the horse-barn was the hog-pen; and lastly, to the outer part of the family stead, there touched the chicken and geese coops. Unitary homes preserved and extended both human and animal heat, a preservative of warmth so vital for human/animal sustenance when fuel was yet a dire lack. In general, Christina Steinert grew up in advanced standards, and tonight she lets her more educated husband know; she reflects with a grain of humor. Tonight she has hope for a more roomy home. The Bitterman home with a kitchen, parlor and two bedrooms made things look better.

It was a Spring that enlivened a move toward expectancy for better times for the Nehers. The Bittermans had removed most of their property except for some of their animals. Included on the Court House sales-note was the purchase of five horses. Some cattle and hogs that belonged to Bittermans were left for disposal.

Dadee and I walked to the prospective home, carrying the lunch pail and a half-gallon syrup pail filled with milk. The five horses were harnessed and hitched to the two-share plow. The furrows divided the field into dark and light strips. The birds flocked about in search of earth-worms and I ran along the furrow with great delight, imitating and aiding the search for any kind of crawlers. Dadee didn't mind me taking off my shoes as I scampered about in the cool furrows. But as curiosity would have it, I wandered back to the yard by the hog-pen where grunter-boar took my attention. The hog had burrowed out of the sty and was grunting as in agony. Trusting animals, I gave way to foolish boldness. I poked a stick at the ferocious boar. Then with a grunt of "oint,oint", in fierce reaction, he darted toward me ... I was never so close to becoming a torn-up piece of human flesh as that day. A sudden sideward move saved me. My heart fluttered. Out of curious venture, the final result could have been tragic. There's nothing stupid about a violent boar.

On the same day another familiar animal made his appearance. It seemed the animals sensed the change. The bull of the cow-herd strived for the yard. The lone bull scratched dry dirt into the air with his clavate foot. With head up or down, and with a low, mooing sound, he'd summon a signal, with the call to the cow or to threaten the by-stander. I picked up a stringent horse-weed and dared closer. I guess to stir up action. Dadee came racing from the field, shouting the danger and forcefully pushing me to a counter-point. And at that point, I received a swatting I've never forgotten. Henceforth the boar and the bull ruled their grounds and I became more conscious of the danger signals, especially of the dominant male animal.

Moving to the second home did not happen at a consecutive time. Field work was the priority. On a rainy day Dadee and Momee painted the inside of the house ... the ceilings, an indigo blue and the floors, a brilliant orange. The Bittermans had the outside of the house painted a murky dark green. I could pick out the striking blue and brilliant orange colors in a rainbow, but the gloomy green color could only be seen in the horrendous clouds that touched the buttes at the horizon to the northwest.

These first days at the new place were rather terrifying. A strangeness overshadowed the family. For Elza and me especially. I could not stand Elza crying, so I ran up the nearby hill and watched a front of dreadful clouds swirl closer. I heard a distress command to get into the house. For the first time in my young life could I look out of a north window and observe the common northwest-brewing thunderstorm. In the sod-house there were no north windows. Up to this point I had never feared a thunderstorm. But this one was different. As the thunder bolted a sudden discharge and the house shook, I slouched down and let out a yelp. Even seeing Momee frightened threw the whole family into a state of insecurity. We all were close to a panic except Dadee.

The storm raged violently. We felt a threatening rumble. Sheets of rain mixed with hail battered the house. An outcry resulted: "Let's go home to our home!" The sod-house never manifested such threat ... not ever. As the fierceness of the thunderstorm subsided we crawled into strange beds. It was Momee's remedy to calm her disturbed brood. Even Dadee seemed troubled because Elza wanted to go where her kittens were.

Two beds were fitted into the west bedroom ... a better bed where Dadee and Momee slept, and a dilapidated bed which the Bittermans had left there. To the Nehers any kind of a bed could be put to use. A folded robe gave the sagging spring a bit of levelness and a rustling foliage-filled mattress caressed the two sleepers, Elza and Paulie. It was the first time I remember sleeping with only one sister. This night I longed for my older sisters so I could cuddle in between them. I needed their sensual warmth.

Three sisters slept in the tiny west bedroom, Dilda, Odeela with Louiza in the middle. The baby boy slept in a cradle which was shoved close to where Momee slept. He bawled and bawled. Whether he felt the thunderstorm pressure, or the discomfort of the tight navel band, or the excitement of the move, is still to be determined. Momee was very tired and upset. Elza was sucking her thumb and sobbing intermittently. Dadee went outside, obviously reflecting on the whim of the storm and gathering courage. I lay there, bewildered, and longing to be back in the sod-house.

It was too wet to work in the field the next morning; Dadee sensitively bid the two most homesick little girls to join him for the last load of homestead stuff that needed to be hauled to the unfamiliar home. Elza and I held hands and waddled over to the empty sod-barn to fetch the mother cat and her young ones. The mother-mouser appeared affected by Elza's absence. There's been no milk in the basin. As we entered the stall mother-cat dropped the sparrow-bird feed. She meowed her way directly over to Elza, slithering about her legs as if to ask: "Where were you?" I carried the three baby-kittens that were nestled in a box and Elza carried the dark-gray mother-cat over to the wagon. Dadee lifted the children-and-cat baggages onto the wagon. A confused and puzzled two-some kids we were. We didn't like this move. Even the cat meowed as if baffled. Why couldn't we have stayed where we used to go to sleep ... in the sod-house home?

These were busy days. Dadee hardly slept. As dawn broke, he made it known it was time for the chores. Momee struck a match and lit the wood-banked stove so to cook the grits and warm the milk for the baby. The boy wailed lustily for attention. It was my early morning duty to rock the cradle. The jolts were pretty hard and yet he bawled. Momee came to my rescue ... unpinned the wet garb and nicely took a hold of a dry blanket-corner and shoved it under him. She had half-filled a lamb-size feeding bottle with warm milk and distended a black rubber nipple onto the bottle, then showed me how to feed him. Well, whatever! I didn't like the drudgery. But neither did Dilda and Odeela like their hard initiation to milking. They were both children and yet were expected to draw milk by hand from the cow's udder. Naturally the effort to milk strengthened their arms and hands, but to see a little girl next to a big cow struggling to milk appeared to be an incredible picture. So were the pioneer children trained, far too early in their lives, for work.

The chore of gathering twigs along the creek and dry manure slabs in the north night-pasture had to be done in haste. Momee found the wood box and 'mischt' (manure) pail empty. The bread had to be baked and to heat the oven, fuel was needed. So many things were missing. Everything was unfamiliar.

It was a chore I readily agreed to. What a jaunt! I ran along swiftly, barefooted. The gumbo patches gloated their annual array. The cactus were in full bloom. The showy flower attracted and rudely enough, one bare foot and both hands received prickers that happens to reckless daring. Dilda appeared for a double rescue. She scanned the area for firewood, replenished the wood-box and came leaping back where her tear-filled sister sat pulling out what stickers her shaky fingers could grasp. Dilda used a large safety pin to dig out the perforated spine on a 'hit-or-miss' poke. I yelled, but the child-doctor rallied: "Here it is, a long sticker!" She promptly spit on the bleeding fissure. I have no knowledge of further complications. The spit-secretion must have been the early-day antibiotic. So the old mother's tale that a baby's "kindes brei" (pappy) must be swished in a mother's mouth before it was fed to the tiny babe. Another one of a midwife's many theories. Human saliva must have been deemed a medical substance. Gags!

More land! Therefore the necessity arose for more horse power. Cow-herding became necessary so to guard the open grain-fields. To keep the cows from invading the lush fields took more than a child's run. A pony was the solution.

Dadee made his way to Jack Crowley, a neighbor-rancher and a horse-dealer. Mr. Crowley sold horses, mostly the halter-broken and on the terms for later payment on the buyer's word of honor. This day Neher begged Crowley for a tamed horse so his little girls could ride him. In contrition

Crowley gave in, not to benefit the demanding "rooshen", rather in simple concern for safe-guarding Neher's little children-workers.

"Call him 'Jack', to Jack Crowley's honor of giving in," mused Dadee. Jack, the horse, had no pony-shape ... rather that of a draft-type. His broad back had plenty ground to hover on and suitable for little girls to learn the action of bare-back riding. Not a more patient horse could have been had than Jack. Mr. Crowley realized he had given up a worthy horse. In a moment of compassion he relented.

Reason had it for a reason. My quickest of ventures at Farm #2 led me to mounting atop Jack. I would rub his neck and head and talk ... then Jack would lean to gentle moves. Jack gave no signs of partiality among the three oldest of Neher girlies. We learned the knack of holding on to Jack's mane, however an abrupt side-aim would give the young rider a sliding off and a thump on prairie's lot. Jack knew when to trot and when to hoof gently over a stony plot, as though he felt the fragile parcel atop him. Jack was ridden daily. The manner of his straight-forward course to round up the cows pleased Dadee. Jack was more than a horse. He had special sense for little girls.

Spring-time advanced. Dadee realized that the herd of cows and calves had to be branded as well as dehorned. And bull-calves castrated. The verminous and fly period would soon be here, causing the animals to be infested. The timely round-up gradually arrived at the Matt Crowley premises. The men did the tortuous act of castrating, dehorning and branding. My sister and I were leaning over on the post-lined corral, observing and listening to the moo-cry of each calf and cow. The calf bawled because it hurt.

At precise timing, the Crowley's hired girl, Martha Grumm, appeared on the scene. She brought with her an enamel dish-pan into which were tossed the bull-calf's testicles, supposedly an ethnic meat dish considered a delicacy. Peeking at all that stuff and feeling with the agony of the animals, I got sick to my stomach. Miss Grumm led me over to the ranch home and stirred up a fizzy drink with hammer-soda. I wondered who suffered most, the calf with its mutilated parts dabbed with turpentine, or I, as the bitter soda drink reached my upset stomach.

Enroute home we passed the dear old homestead. I pleaded with Dadee to let the cows go back to the real home-yard. What a passionate hurt to pass it by! As we drove the fatigued herd into the night pasture, I darted up the hill and sat on a stone, gazing inattentively over the valley wherein lay our new environment. I cried. The day was hard. These hills didn't suit the distraught and homesick waylayer. I longed to go to the home --- where the sod-walls were molded with loam!

Wash day perhaps was the hardest work-day of the week for the pioneer woman. There were no washing machines. Instead, tubs, rub-boards and boilers; the home-made soap (made from fats and lye) and water were the main untensils and ingredients needed. Family members, mostly the woman and girls, did the lug, rub and wring. Fortunate were the families which had good wash-water.

The Nehers had it not easy for wash-water ... at neither home. Both wells pumped up hard water that tinged the wash. Momee was particular about her wash. Rain water was collected in barrels or hauled to home from a still water-pool or river. During winter snow had to be thawed.

On a Sunday evening a large boiler kettle was placed on the kitchen stove and filled with suitable water for a Monday wash-day. All the dirty clothes were sorted according to color and grime. For the average family, ten to fifteen piles was the ordinary.

After outdoor chores and milk separator and breakfast dishes were washed, Monday's wash-day duties began. The spotted or dirtier clothes were soaked in cool water for a few minutes. Each item was rubbed on a washboard with a daub from a bar of home-made lye soap. The white wash had to be gently submerged into the boiler and revolved with a broom handle and simmered a bit. Then removed and rinsed in a tub of cold water that had been tinged with Lydia Pinkham's blueing. Next, wrung out by hand. The special dress clothes and handiwork received starching.

Unfortunately not all back-yards claimed a wash-line. The garden or cow fence displayed a line of clothes with the barb-wire taking the place of clothes pins. Along with a strong wind, what additional mending the over-worked mother got! So, also, were the young, growing girls taxed with arduous labor. Every girl who could reach over the wash-board had her turn at rubbing clothes. And lugging the soap-water to the chicken coop was an end-wash-day job. So to splash the walls that helped kill chicken lice. Oh, of course, the kitchen and porch floors had to be scrubbed. Along about then, evening chores called for doing.

If it was a school day, likely one of the older girls had to stay home and help Mother, as she taught her the art of washing clothes the proper way. Even starching and sprinkling the wash required special instruction. No school subject was deemed as important as learning to do the wash the right way.

The pioneer-woman was judged on whether she was a good or bad homemaker on how the dish towels looked and how wrinkle-free her wash was. Even though she had no ironing board and had to iron the wash on a padding that lay flat on the kitchen table, she managed to iron most all of the wash ... clothes, dish-towels as well as bedding.

Tuesday generally was the 'ironing day'. This meant building a hot fire on hot days and heating the sad-irons on top of the stove. The ironer removed one iron at a time with a wooden-handled clamp, using it for a few pieces of wash ... then she would exchange it for iron #2. It took three sad-irons for steady ironing and several pails full of the lighter fuel for a day of ironing. The same day the heated oven baked loaves and loaves of delicious ever-lasting yeast bread. A woman's worth depended on how much and how well she could do the thousand tasks that beckoned. Her work required to render services both indoors and outdoors. And the making of everything from scratch. It, too, being her duty to teach and train her daughters in like manner.

The reality of frightful times the pioneers had, as they emigrated from one unknown to another, was true. There were unexpected and mysterious happenings. Imagine living in a wilderness, away from civilization: Indian scares, wild animal packs, Nature's forces, accidents, illnesses, and on and on. A good part of conversations centered around scary tales and the predictions of omens. Women and children depended on the men for security. A man's dream had more certainty toward something happening than a woman's vision.

Weather signs, superstitions, and omens resulted from occurrences. A lot of predictions and prophecies were foretold. And, 'by gosh', you believed them, especially if a man told them.

Life in the beginning at the north-home had already lessened our security. It's not been a comfortable beginning. I remember Dadee getting up one night and going to the barn. With the aid of a lantern he checked on a cow. It was pitch dark. As he returned to the house, the rooster crowed in full alarm. Next morning during breakfast Dadee predicted that something not good might happen; or, the rooster's crow is an omen for bad news.

Well, something 'not-so-good' did happen! A two-horse rake runaway! Dealing with half-broken horses, runaways were common. The rooster crowed because he saw the lantern light. To him it was the morning sun and time to call the "wake-up!"

As a young girl I relished the chore of gathering eggs and feeding the chickens. The mysterious excitement of a rooster's crow and the cackle of a hen after laying an egg enlivened my whole being. I wanted to sound along. It pleased me to be able to scatter feed and stand in the middle of grain-peckers. The closer the flock surrounded me, the more ecstatic I got.

All the little chicks were hatched under a row of setting-hens. At a corner of the barn-loft, or by a granary partition, nests were carved round in the straw-filled boxes. Between twelve and fifteen choice eggs were placed into the handmade nest. Then in the evening when the broody-hens were well in a dazed condition, we carried them carefully to the fake nests. Another box was placed over each cluck to confine and get her adjusted. Not every 'cluck' took to the new environment. She would abandon the foreign nest and harry about the barn upstairs. The next evening we tried another brooder. The intent to set a row of about ten hens that hovered the nests of eggs for a numerous hatch. A bowl of water and a spread of grain provided easy feed. A Spring spectacle lining a hay-loft!

It took exactly three weeks of a broody-hen's body warmth until chicks began to crack the shells and free themselves from cramp. After most of the chicks were hatched, the bare-hen would succumb to a terrible fuss, clucking and pecking at whomever reached for the 'young-uns'! Momee would select three well-feathered and the more patient kind as the Mother-hens ... the chicks were distributed and the instinctive 'cluck' hovered a protection that is indescribable. The rest of the degenerated hens were given their free flutter. What a wage!

The excitement for any child to behold the natural hatching process and to hold a fluffy little chick in the palm instilled a life-long sedative for bird-love as well as an aversion for the grown chicks to be butchered for food.

Perhaps no other pests have menaced the pioneers during the summer season as the flies. Man and animals suffered acutely. Swarms of hideous and annoying flies thronged every kitchen and separator room, every pen and barn and moved about where food and feed was; the pests would settle on animals as well as human beings, causing great irritation as well as mental and physical pain. No worse pathetic scene could be perceived than a helpless baby lying in a cradle covered with black crawlers. Nothing more enraging that could have happened to the milker as when Bossie kicked and tossed the pail of frothy milk over him/her. Bossie didn't mean to milk-bathe her serf ... what the tail-swat couldn't do, the kick had to ward off. The stings could be intolerable.

I truly deem the early-day "fly-time" as the number-one threat to both health and comfort. Screen windows and screened doors were a scarcity. Chemical sprays were yet unknown. Sticky runners hanging on ceilings or black-poison fly-paper, sprinkled with sugar and wetted down, specked the tables and floors with dead flies. Occasionally a child would die before the flies got the die-taste. Even so with the cream that was hauled to the market, the creamery man would sieve out a good number of black flies ... and in casual town gossip pass on his advice: "Why don't the farm-wives buy the Tanglefoot Sticky Fly Paper?"

The long shed at the north-home was converted into a summer kitchen and a milk separator room. It had no screening the first year. Momee, a neat woman, covered the freshly baked sugar kuchens with dish towels and yet the large, black flies got in, as happened on every baker's table. Hence cometh the anecdotes of 'fly-specked kuchen'.

Flies, flies, flies! They were the disease carriers; they were the summer season's menace!

Roads leading to outer fields, or to neighbors, meandered around and about hills, stones, pot-holes and creeks ... wherever Dadee guessed it best for wagon or buggy driving, he devised the route. Muddy roads were in no way easily driven. I can still hear the sucking sounds those horse hooves made as the horses pulled free from an occasional knee-deep hole. Traveling was a risk, even moreso with a buggy. If the buggy sagged toward the edge of a vertical cliff, we held on for dear life. We had visions of us rolling down the hill, buggy and all. And horses were unpredictable. We lived through many harrowing experiences with our horses. After all, no two horses were alike. A temperamental horse could exhibit a speed at her own fast rate; the next horse would hold back at the expense of a broken tug. The team could have been trained with each other well ahead of time, but if something suddenly frightened them, they could gallop out of control and create an unfortunate happening. Especially if both horses were the sensitive type.

Bay, the homestead-horse, had developed a stiffness. She was no longer fit for a buggy-hitch. Dadee matched one of the Bitterman horses, Querly, to Jack, the draft-horse pony. Dressed in our Sunday best, the five oldest Neher children settled in the back box-type part of the buggy. Momee held the baby and sat next to Dadee on an elevated, topped front seat. The buggy was loaded. Querly inclined this morning to tenseness, probably due to a barometrical pressure following a thunderstorm. Hardly started with the drive, Querly was up on his hind legs. Dadee controlled the hectic drive. Naturally we were all scared. Little did we realize that a worse scare was at hand. We were on our way to Sunday School.

Following the Saturday night downpour, the regular creek-way had surged up to a flood-stage by Sunday morning. After investigating the situation, Dadee 'giddy-yapped' the horses to go. Jack bucked the venture, but Querly darted at a ghastly pace across the frothing waters. I hardly think the buggy wheels touched the bottom of the stream-bed. We were splashed with water and shock, but safe. Querly demonstrated super horse-sense. Henceforth Dadee made Querly and Jack the mainstay-team. Whatever other horse was handy had to do for pony service. And the naive and daring Paulie entrusted any horse for to round up the cows, with no casualty to speak of.

During the month of June the average prairie-land farmer began to excavate the ground off of the coal vein, so that coal could be dug and hauled home for winter's fuel. This year Dadee had one of the Martin boys manage the team of horses that were hitched to a single scraper. The blade of the scraper was raised and lowered by the operator, then measured for the grade by his expert guess. George held the lines and Dadee managed the rig with two handles, horses abreast and going round and round, dragging up dirt to level ground. Occasionally one horse would end in a down-slide to the bottom of the coal chasm. Dadee untangled the horses and bluntly shouted out his tension. Those were moments of fright!

After the removal of dirt, the coal had to be chopped loose with pick or blasted loose with dynamite. It tested man's endurance to a frazzle and weighed heavily on both animals' and man's energies. To chop up, load up, drive it home and unload ... unhitch, water and feed and unharness the horses, the coal-digger turned out the horses, 'get yourselves a roll', as he wearily walked to the water tank, dipping his soot/sweat-covered head way into it and swishing the grime aside, as in a moment of freshness, he sounded out: "Mutter, mir hen ja koala; ich will was zum essa!" (Mother, we have coals; I want something to eat!)

The first summer's feed and grain harvest on the north-home fared well. Nature dealt well with the Nehers. One hailstorm went through the Elm Creek area and hacked down an oat-field which was a feed loss.

Dadee, a fast-pace man, hardly slept. I see him sharpening the grass-mower's blades during noon-hour, biking the wheel, precisely holding the blade for a brisk cutting edge and sweat dripping down his forehead. Done with the blade, he stooped over and laid down in the shade of the granary ... his head resting on a folded gunny sack. The sweat-rimmed hat perched on his face to keep the flies away; hands folded on his chest, shoes off, and snoring away. From sweat, his feet gave off a bad smell. After all, Dadee has been up and racing around since dawn broke. The orders to his family would be preceded by a whistle, which became characteristic. Dadee was a hard worker and a hard trainer as well.

His girl-children had to be trained into chores and taught common sense for which Dadee had hardly time for, and least of all, had patience for. We were children, although forced into responsibilities beyond ability. Especially Dilda and Odeela. For the work lay at hand and it had to be done. Let's remember, all the overseeing hung heavily on Dadee.

There was so much to be done and all depended on the energies of man, woman, children and horse. Haying and harvesting stood at hand. A new way of life is everywhere. The yard beckoned with life: two colts, a number of calves, piggies, chicks, goslings ... and a baby 'boi', Edwin, who wailed for attention! A mixture of exuberance and strain prevailed in the Neher yard!

I am sensing that my care-free childhood days are over. I was being pressured with more and more commands. There wasn't free time to loiter around the hills, as I had done in the beloved prairie-home, there where life was a bliss!

A strangeness comes over me. It's harder to walk barefoot all day in this peculiar yard. And through sharp stubble on the field Dadee has mowed for hay. Some even cut the skin on my legs, causing trickles of blood which drew the flies. They sting me and I cry. It is nothing to my sisters when I show it to them, because they too have their troubles. They have to work as full-grown girls. I see Dadee loading up the hay rack, forkful after forkful of the season's fresh hay, driving it by the stack and instructing Dilda and Odeela to pitch the hay from the rack onto the stack ... while Momee was forming and setting the haystack. In the meantime Dadee unhitched and hitched the horses onto a rake, so to bunch the hay for the next loading.

I had to run errands and watch the baby as well. I'm reminded of having to fill the gunny-cloth-covered jug with fresh water, lugging it out to the field, and fetching it in a hurry. Heat is everywhere. Even 'der hund' pants for breath. I'm weary and hot and am hardly able to carry the jug into a hole by the bottom of the stack, where the cool ground keeps the water cool. Everybody holds the jug high and drinks lustily out of the jug spout. Dadee drinks first. Then, one by one, the others follow. I drink last. It's a funny taste to my sensitive mouth. Something like a saltiness. I could smell offensive odor. Likely the distaste from everybody's mouth. Oh, I longed to cup the water to drink from a creek-hole! Behind the hill of our 'bestest' home!

Our entire life on the new home is changing. More land, more stock, more family ... all this meant more work. And with the added work-world, Dadee had to add to the machinery list.

With harvesting at hand, Dadee obtained a second-hand header. He gloated over this immense, new-fangled machine, especially when he witnessed the smooth works of wheat stalks dropping neatly backward onto the cradle-bed, and a shimmering ribbon coming out of the elevator. "So was hen mir niemols kat in Russland!" (We never had anything like this in Russia!) Dadee boasted. Five horses were hitched to a rear apparatus with a man standing on a raised surface, handling and manipulating horses and machine. As the machine was guided into a ripe, golden grain field, Dadee set it to cutting. The neat stream of grain that lay on the header-canvas then conveyed up the elevator, and fell into the header-box. Dilda, who could hardly see over the front slant of the rack, was expected to drive the rack-team at an even pace with the header, or a freak thing could happen ... the grain being spewn on the ground. Or, the hayrack and elevator result in a breakage.

Momee stands in the rack with fork and hustles to clear away the wheat that is falling on her. It piles up and Dadee slows down. We've gone through a vale where the stand was thick. My, what massive, golden, filled-out heads this field is producing! Dadee, laughing, after the rack was filled to overflowing, gleefully remarked: "Mir griegen viel waitza schteck; ihr maedla griegen yedes aa wenter-kidel ... wenner fleisich schaffen." (We will have many wheat stacks; each of you girls will get a winter coat ... if you work attentively.)

It was a searing hot day. Clothes clung wet to our bodies. There's not much time for rest. Dadee is watching the clouds to the west. He does not want a hailstorm to touch the fields. So we move steadily on.

A short time before harvesting Momee poured a can of malt into a large crock, added lukewarm water and yeast. Each morning she would reach into the sugar bowl and grab as much sugar as could be taken up and sprinkled it into the liquid substance. How it would sizz! There in the corner of the summer-kitchen next to the cast-iron stove, stood the brew for beer. Momee would allow it to ferment for days. I had to wash the bottles. Momee filled them and we girls wangled the stomper, pushing on a bottle-cap. As we felt a thud and grip, we knew it was tight. Then stored in the cool cellar for a bit of aging. Here was beer for harvesting. "Ach, dez isch ja so goot wens haiz isch." (Oh, that is so good when it's so hot.) Dadee surmised that drinking beer prevented the outbreak of boils behind his neck. Pumping cold well-water into a pail containing several bottles of home-made beer and brought to the harvesters quenched a thirst and vigorized the tired. In later years home-made root beer became a summer's beverage. To have a beer on a hot day inclined for more sustenance.

Everybody had to help during harvesting. A woman's place usually was on a hay or grain stack, shaping it according to instructions from her man. Likely she left a baby in the care of an older child, occasionally with sad results ... as when the babe would smother or choke.

Baking bread during the night was not uncommon during harvesting time; so also to pluck several springers for quick frying as well as washing clothes.

There had to be food. The eats had to be made from scratch. Or you had none. One day a rain-shower halted the headering. While Dadee unhitched and unharnessed the horses, Momee started a fire in the cast-iron stove, so to heat water in the boiler in preparation for the scalding of a young hog that was to be butchered. I see Dadee sharpening the butcher-knife and at an alternate glance, size up one of the 'piggies'. I was sensitive to the butchering act and would run behind the barn, leaning to feeling; a writhing pity for the piggies.

I would not show up for the following steps in the butchering process. Not before the final act. The summer kitchen table was laden with pork-cuts and Momee pressed them, portion by portion, into an eight-gallon cream can, until plumb-full of delicious pork. Dadee tied firmly a long rope to the cream can handles, according to his typical bind-tie, and then extended the container of meats way down to the water level of the second well ... then securely tied the rope to a foothold. To pull up or let down the heavy can took precision and careful handling on the part of two young girls. "You do it and don't you drop it!" was the order. We had many a meal of fresh, young pork for noon eats. Not ever was there spoilage! This was a farmer's one way for refrigeration; another way, by pumping cold water into a container and setting the bottled drinks into it; or plunging a few watermelons into one-half a barrel-full of cold water.

Yet, the main manner of cooling and preserving foods was the earthen-dug cellars where food was set directly into an underground dugout on the cold ground surface. Root-cellars, often a separate, peaked-roofed structure in the yard, implied prosperity. A stone-lined and board-enforced ladder, leading way down into a hollowed-out room, took human slavery labor to get the dirt up ... room enough to store a winter's supply of vegetables, kraut and lard crocks and barrels of pickles. What a lugging of stuff it took, up and down!

Nothing was easy. Food for the family had to be made from a starting place by means of hand; every mode of building required hard labor; every field brought to productivity challenged the energy of horse and man. It was many years before I realized that my father's and mother's courage and hard work were enduring evidence of undaunted pioneers ... they who taught us that 'arbeit macht das leben suez!" (Work addeth a sweet reward to life!)

The Deep Creek had been a constant bewilderment for me during the cattle-herding times. The new hills east of the north-home, appeared rather frightening to us three older girls. There was something strange about the wildlife as well as the general formation of the region. It reflected a sort of an eerie feeling because of its precarious wildness. The hill-range to the northeast was composed of banded badlands with gumbo patches dotting the base ground. Here cactus blooms added a bit of beauty in the ruggedness of its surroundings. "In the creviced rifts you'll find a shelter for snakes," Dadee said. True enough, the Prairieland children feared snakes. Naively we forgot the warnings and eventually ventured the whole area.

The Deep Creek valley was designated for cattle-herding. It was mainly Odeela's and my job to guard the cows from going astray. Jack, the draft-horse pony, was needed for fallow-work, therefore the two of us were expected to outrun the cows in the case of a cow-chase. Cows frequently became restless, especially when a thunderstorm was brewing ... then they would run hither and thither. Or if flies threatened the cows into a run. Which meant we two young girls had to cover every hilltop slope and creek to re-direct the course of the herd. Barefooted, we boldly ran about the risky parts of the cliffs. "Der hund' scampered near about. Suddenly Odeela screamed. She saw a snake coil about and exert a rattle. Odeela ran aside and the old dog approached in time to take up the feud. I stood boldly nearby and sicked the dog to attack. And he gave a dog's doggedness. Two scared kids drove the cows home and stammered the feudal scene. Dadee investigated and found 'der hund' faintly yapping with unusual spasms. 'Der hund' died from the snake poison. He gave his all to protect the innocent. Dadee buried our faithful dog in a natural hollow near about where he died. We children were overtaken with a sadness mixed with fear. The riddle of dog departure held a deprived loneliness. 'Der hund' was gravely missed.

The Deep Creek held in its range a bit of everything. It was like stepping into a different world. Something like a fantasy. The forked creeks lined with native foliage and trees made way to a middle deep creek running from north to south and gradually spilling into the Knife River.

The Burkhardt plateau lay to the east and a longated hill to the west where every kind of wild fruit trees and bushes grew and produced chokecherries, the wild plum and Juneberries. The buffalo berry patch had its own bounded slope. At the foothill the gooseberry bush thrived. An isolated mulberry bush favored edible berries and ground cherries could be found along prairie's ridges. Rose hips and the buffalo berry were luscious after Jack Frost savored them. The Indian breadroot (Indian potato) was an important food tuber for cow herders. During the entire cow-herding season, the Deep Creek offered nutriment for human and animal hunger. Its fruition times yielded in alternate order. Nature produced and preserved in an effective manner. Each season offered its produce but the summer and autumn seasons gloated its abundance.

This natural valley-region, composed of various soils, held one select spot for a watermelon patch. Or shall we call it an 'outer-garden'. Needless to say, Dadee took great pride in being able to raise the biggest and sweetest watermelons. It seemed as though there was something of a challenge among the neighbors to outdo each other's watermelon superbness.

Here by southeast slant of a northward hill Dadee broke up the fertile soil for an 'outer garden'. It lay next to the road leading through the Deep Creek, a bit out of view from the farmstead. After a summer evening of milking, the family gathered by the patch with Dadee stepping carefully among the entwined vines, investigating, snapping and feeling the special watermelon and admonishing us kids not to invade the patch. We were taught to pull and hoe weeds and to pick bugs off of the potato plants, but not to enter the melon plot unless he gave permission. Dadee reigned by way of brief orders.

We were no better than other kids. Born with the initial sin, we not only tramped the vines, we sized up Dadee's special melon and used a pocket knife to cut a deep-edged square out of the bottom of the melon ... to investigate for ripeness. After finding it barely in a pink tint, the seeds still whitish, we pushed the fragment back in and turned the watermelon to its original position ... thus, a gradual ooze soaked the good earth with a sweetness that drew an ant colony. Odeela and I were the marauders. We were tempted to eat of this one special watermelon, just as Eve was at the Garden of Paradise. She had to eat of the forbidden apple. Eve suffered for her sin, and Odeela and I did too. The evil was easily discovered. After a few more hot days, Dadee checked his prime melon, thinking perhaps that by now it would have the right snap. He looked at the ringlet which curled against the melon ... yes, that had turned brown, indicating a ripeness. Dadee snapped and lifted the melon ... it was light and lifeless. What followed was the procedure most of the early-day children were raised by. Odeela blamed it onto me and I, on her. I doubt if the spanks stopped the melon-prickers. Hereafter drained watermelons showed up in every neighbor's patch. After all, the craving to crack a melon on one's knee had to undergo a test first!

The watermelon patches always received uncommon visitors ... the kind that invaded just before dawn. Following a dog's explosive bark, the prowler was frightened to a run by way of a gun-shot! Oh, for the watermelon patch akin to the road meandering through the Deep Creek!

The Deep Creek depicted a wide range on interests in meadowy grass and foliage, in animal and bird life, as well as in its rugged image ... a kind of prairieland specter that took my focus. It eased my homesickness for the homestead-hills. Even if part of it denoted it as of a terrifying nature.

In fact we girls enjoyed a kind of a secret plot that offered play-time. As we herded cattle we settled by way of the south entry where it was comfortable.

The little hill, dotted with a buffalo berry patch, was a look-out top to keep watch on the grazing cows. A meadowlark pair raised its young with our company; a hawk cried a noisy crow as she swerved overhead to warn us against molesting the twiggy nest in a lone tree; a vale, where Nature intended for trees to grow for more shade and allow a squirrel to scold the invader; where birds sang in full encore and wild flowers took turns in presenting an array color express; where we could listen to a trickle patter urging a tiny waterfall that made its way into a flowing brook ... that is, after a Spring thaw or a Summer's shower! The south setting of the Deep Creek displayed a safeness.

A little way up were clay patches where we devised a form of a household. We dug into a prairie bank and shaped it into a room, pretending it was our sod-made abode. We placed rows of little stones, creating imaginary rooms and furnishings were made of prairie-twigs and such. We cut out catalogue characters. We snitched bits of cloth, pins, nails and whatever took our fancy ... from around and about the home. Eventually the outfield play-house dulled our responsibility duties. Scheck, the leader-cow, led the other cows into a lush oats field. We heard Dadee shout. The damage, after the night-shower was extensive. Dakee realized that no one could outrun Scheck!

After many decades ago, I hike about the Secret Place, sit on a familiar stone, and look over the Deep Creek that taught us lessons for responsibility and character. And the rare play-times!

These were critical days. A sudden thrust of added burdens. Dadee wondered if he should have taken on the extra hilly domain. He was ill at ease with the prevailing problems. He realized that his barefooted girls could not control the fly-afflicted cows. There was a need for a steady pony and a reliable dog, and animals had to be trained. Neither was human help sufficient.

Scheck, the roamer-cow, had to be yoked. Dadee nailed together a yoke during late evening hours, something like a heavy, wooden cross-piece enclosing the head of an animal. What a struggle to get that thing on! But Scheck slowed her straying. At least for the time being.

The hay mower, with a cut-bar in front of two wheels, was hitched to a team of horses. On the elevated seat, right behind the horses, is where Dadee sat. The oats field which the cows messed needed cutting. A stone was hidden under the laid-over oats and in no way could it be detected. The cut-bar pierced into the rock with a screeching sound that excited the horses. To hold the team in line and bring them to a back-up took minute precision of handling. Lady hoisted ahead and then up! Mike backed up and almost rested his haunch on Dadee's lap. Obviously it turned out to be a nerve-frazzling experience.

The same field had to be raked. The hay rake, a wonder apparatus, held a center-seat with tines of circular shape made for gathering together the mowed hay, then dumping it in straight rows. Dilda, a young teenager, sat on the rig's seat and took on this dangerous work to drive the horses as well as stepping the lever, regulating for straight rows. Dadee hitched trusting Jack with another slow-gaited horse and gave Dilda orders on how to do it. It was Jack the horse that used sense in protecting prairieland's little girls. Both in riding as well as in driving. In too many ways, pioneer children were not properly prepared, nor ready either emotionally or physically, to do the varied farm labor. Children were raised for work. Such logic was brought over from the old countries. And there was a reason for it. The raising of crops for a livelihood depended on human and animal energy. In a broad sense, the life of peasantries demanded that type of work from man, woman and child. The prairie settlers, collectively speaking, desired more land, to prove a man's worth who has money in his 'geld beutel' (purse). A land-hungry man hinged his progress on a working family.

Uncle Fred Martin had the fortune of having boys who could work and in the meantime he could spend his time and efforts figuring out the ways and means of using and adapting the latest machinery into service, whereas Dadee faced these critical tasks of having to be everywhere, practically alone. His lot was understandably hard. Mowing, bunching, hauling and stacking hay; headering, stacking threshing, shoveling grain onto a wagon and hauling it eighteen miles by the horse-drawn method — to the Hebron Mill — for flour. A portion of the grain had to be sold for ready cash to make payments on the many bills that Dadee, the lone farmer, promised to pay. "Ja, ja," the businessman would say, as he opened a drawer and removed a rubber band from a rolled-up pile of paper slips. Herr Urban put on his 'specs' and sought out Neher's bill. "Ich kann net alles bezahla, aber etwas davon kann ich!" (I can't pay everything, but some of it I can!) "Wenn nur alle leute so ehrlich wären zum bezahlen, dock mit nur etwas von der schuld!" (If only all people would be honest enough to pay only a portion of their debt!) Dadee and Herr Urban shook hands: "Danke, danke, Gott sei mit dir!" (Thanks, thanks, God be with you!) So spoke Herr Urban.

 Quite frequently I was favored to join Dadee on a load of grain to town. The above scene has given me a lasting impression ... a business deal between a high German and a low German! I remember seeing my father giving way to a temper as prairieland's trials overwhelmed him, but deep down he dealt with honesty and this day, on our drive homeward, Dadee seemed pleased. Could it be he felt a lift for the praise he had received from Herr Urban?

Very likely during summer time a rimmed, wooden barrel sat close to the well and was kept full of water. One hot afternoon I undressed completely and swished in the forbidden water. With no inkling, the Carl Bauer family drove into the yard. I kept my head down as Mr. Bauer watered his horses. In a jovial way Mr. Bauer reached into the barrel and took a hold of my hair. I scurried out of the barrel and streaked up to the barn with no clothes. I've never forgotten the embarrassment. You see, little girls were taught modesty. It was not decent to show any naked part of a body ... especially not a girl. We girls, at our home, were so shy about our nude bodies. We would dress and undress with our clothes made into a tent over our heads.

We had no bathing suits in our days of growing up. We wore older dresses or, for sure, a pair of bloomers, as we darted either into a dam, river or creek's pond. We knew not more but that nudeness was a shame. To keep growing children unaware of menstrual and sexual facts ruled as a virtuous thing among parents. Hardly ever was there ever anything explained. "The less they know, the better!" An adage.

We were left to discover and learn of the dangers about and around us, much too much, without explanation. Like wading or diving into a dam or river without a hint for swimming lessons ... or how to float if the wader hits a hole. "You'll learn if you once start sinking!" Another common remark.

I shudder when I think back. I could not swim, yet in all innocence I ventured or dove into any waters, not realizing the risk I took. Naively stupid. I challenged dare-devil actions. Every barn-peak I was first to peek down from in pride; whether a pony or work-horse, harnessed or unharnessed, I mounted, so to tame it; I guess I should have been yoked, like Scheck was. It must have been God having sent a Guardian Angel to save Prairieland's 'hayseed' so that she may write the story when "The Prairie Was Home!"

The large, one-room schoolhouse of District 21 #2 was located several miles southeast from our north-home near the end of a natural Elm Creek. The brown building was situated next to the play-hill where the pupils abounded in slides, hides and pranks. The schoolyard amply fitted for outdoor games and the eastward road-view revealed many an incident that dealt with early-day life ... like the teacher who came driving in a one-horse-drawn buggy; or Mrs. Matt Crowley out riding her favorite horse; or witnessing the dark smoke rising in bursts from a distant prairie fire. Even a sadder scene was when there passed a funeral procession of buggies and wagons aiming for the cemetery.

The big brown schoolhouse exemplified itself as a perfect country school. Pupils arrived from all directions over hill and vale carrying their buckets that contained the ordinary hunk of chokecherry syrup-soaked bread, a pickle and a piece of meat or sausage. Not much variety. Of course, a bottle of water. If you ran out, the bottle was replenished with creek-hole water.

During my tenure of country-school life, the enrollment at School #2 was at its height ... with forty-some pupils. They were the offspring of Boehlers, Burkhardts, Martins, Nehers, Schnaidts, Schocks and at interval years the Jack Crowley and Matt Crowley children. The most qualified of the two schools received the Crowley children.

School #1, located near the Knife River, was smaller in size and white in color. It was called the Smith school. Children registered from families of the Backfishes, Grumms, Roeslers, Smiths, Salmons and later the Krein children and at alternate times, the Jack and Matt Crowley children. As well as others, in both schools, for short periods of time.

One teacher for all grades. They had a hard role to play: teacher, disciplinarian, janitor, game-playing leader, nurse, musician. He/she had to prove to be of character; he/she had to be religious and patriotic and serve with a very meager wage.

Due to the lack of growing up, size-wise, I was taken as a pre-school child even when I was way past six years. Therefore I was kept from starting school at the proper age. Actually I was needed at home to rock the cradle for the babies that were born, one after another.

I started school in September of 1919 and obviously had been indoctrinated into the German language. I knew very few English words, which was the case for the majority of pupils. The German settlers vied with the English language and seemed determined to contend for superiority. Similar contention disputed churches as well. Teachers, clergymen and neighbors faced this number-one problem with much disagreement. Apparently classing and division among elders and children resulted.

Teachers were commanded to use compulsion. Whips, belts and sticks were used to punish the children who spoke German. School children received severe infliction with little explanation.

During one noon hour, the teacher sat by an open window, crocheting away on a piece of lace, and listening for German talk. Ida Boehler and I were caught expressing ourselves in German. Each of us had to lie face down across the teacher's desk. The repulsive teacher opened the underwear flaps and hit each of us on the bare-bottom with a stick. Ida was first, so I had a chance to think despite my fright. I hung my head down off the edge of the desk and stuck a finger down my throat inducing a good supply of vomit. The cruel teacher added to her duties that of a scrubber-woman. My bottom didn't get it as hard as Ida's.

Another early-Fall school experience that has never evaded my mind happened at the school-yard privy. I had settled on the seat-board on a little hole down low. A bat swooshed down and got entangled in my hair. Mrs. Salmon, the ideal School #2 teacher, put on the coal-mitts and took scissors to the jerky bat, cutting twists of hair to wrestle loose the parasite. Emotions ran high in the schoolroom. A checkered head, how I did sigh ... too much was said, which made me cry!

The horse-and-buggy age has had a sentimental impact on my early life out in the country. Sure, during snow-and-mud covered roads, sleds and wagons were used to go from one place to another; but buggy-driving seemed to be the fair-weather means of transportation.

After a pair of horses were specifically trained for a buggy team, it could be driven by people of any age. School children drove by buggy. The chance of a two-buggy meet shouted the teams, along with a hit of the whip, into a race.

The Martin boys vied with the Schnaidt boys into a buggy contest of speed. The Neher pupils had been picked up shortly before the race began, therefore the Martin buggy was loaded to capacity. A galloping race down the slanting hill! All of us tried to hold on as the buggy wheels whirred vibrantly fast. The Martin and Schnaidt harassers both stood up in the front position of the buggy with legs astride for balance, and slapping the lines on the horses' rumps, flinging the whip and shouting the race. The horses galloped and at the same time retarded the pace. Little Martha Martin took a flying leap over the back part of the buggy and landed flat on her back with a thud that stirred the rest of us to a startled scream. We were aroused and scared. The Martin contender halted the team as the horses shook heads in snorts and then subsided. Martha was picked up and the result was a few uncontrolled tears. Nature did the soothing and healing of hurts in any or all of prairieland's children. Martha was not taken to a doctor. Later in life she attested that that accident may have had something to do with the fact that her brain could not assimilate the multiplication tables which had to be memorized tit for tat.

Some really funny things happened during the buggy era. If a saloon-visitor, after hours of indulgence, 'giddy-yapped' his enduring team toward home and curtly slouched over, one harness-line revolving along near the axle of the wheel, and the other line held fast under the weight of the drunk, he actually arrived home safely. The faithful horses stopped short next to the entrance-gate in front of the house, charging their heads up and down as if to lay the next step of responsibility on the barking dog. The rest of the story you know! Horse sense outweighed a master's ill wit.

Two common time buggy scenes were where the family was driving to a church on a Sunday morning, everyone dressed in their best; and where a school teacher was coming over the hill in a one-horse buggy. Yes, the drivers not only swayed the polished harness lines, they used a fancy buggy whip lightly just to show off. Sometimes a parent or school teacher would use the whip on the unruly type of teenager. I did not like such a scene.

During the later 1800's and the first two decades of the 1900's was the golden age of buggy times ... rolling, rolling on the meandering prairieland roads ... as we huddled together on a buggy, listening to the whir of the wheels, the snort of the horses and the sounding song of the wind! These were the exciting and happy buggy days.

What was early grade-school like at School #2? I can still hear the school bell, a clear, resonant sound to set the reminder for school time. We had been jumping rope, playing hide-and-go-seek, or pump-pump-pullaway. We lined up in a row as we entered the school house. It was mostly the younger children who answered to the roll call. The older sons and daughters were definitely needed at home for early Fall work. To attend school regularly and to abide by certain rules was not yet compulsory.

There were rows and rows of seats and a large round stove occupied a portion of the north wall with the coal shed to the northwest. The teacher's desk could be pushed to the middle of the south entry-doors or to the west, a bit away from the blackboard. The east wall included a row of windows, and two north windows separated far enough for the heater's space. The south entrance accommodated an outer-door with a fixed window on each side. We hung our wraps on nails and set the lunch pails and water bottles on a shelf. The school house was painted brown. A typical country school!

The lower grade school environment held definite impressions that I remembered all my life ... conditions marked by compulsion as well as composure. The psychology used by some of the teachers as well as the dominating parents wasn't all that sensible. Some teachers did the children great good; others were an abomination to the emotional welfare of the children.

Take for example the inability to memorize arithmetic, spelling and readings! Grave punishment often with stick-and-whip thrashes were handed out, definitely in the form of abuse. Children's mental states were beset with fear, therefore thwarted from learning. These were sad theories from ages back.

I hold great respect for Mrs. Salmon, who used a logical manner of teaching and has probably had the greatest effect on my young school life ... as well as on my contemporaries. She explained things. She stood for cleanliness, bringing out the best in each pupil and she stood for moral principles. She believed in opening the school day with a prayer followed by patriotic numbers. District 21, Elm Creek Schools #1 and #2 record Mrs. Dick Salmon as an outstanding country-school teacher. Mrs. Salmon seemed to portray the ability to reason with school children on a reasonable level in disciplining. She believed in letting go of medievalism and making life a learning process toward the pursuit of happiness. She has had great influence on the early grade school years of my life and on other children as well.

(Here-about I close the story of the innocent years of my life. Much has been said, but much remains unsaid. I taxed my subconscious mind to the facts as best I could. Forgive the wrongs and value the rights ... all to remember the benefits of a child scanning the Creator's prairieland!)

The farm took on a working pressure. The list of projects were endless. More buildings needed to be erected or enlarged; fences, to be repaired and extended, but the land had priority. The cycle of plowing, disking, seeding and harrowing was ever on Dadee's mind. The seed had to be in the ground to take advantage of Spring's rain. Everything depended on one man's decisions and doings. Boys' help was missing.

Dilda and Odeela, ten and nine years old, were expected to take on adult responsibilities; Paulie was bold enough to mount any harnessed work horse to gather the cows; Momee was walking slower and slower. The workload became out of proportion for one man. I saw my father sweat-stained, weary and worried. Life was difficult.

On April 11, 1919, Anna was born. Another baby girl delivered by Mutter Lennick with the help of Mutter Burkhardt. The boy Edwin was a little over two years old. It became Louisa's duty to rock the cradle where this baby laid in. I retained a loving impression of Anna's growing up years. She was the "sunshine" child ... a ready smile crowned her whole make-up. She grew up to be a vivacious prairie-roaming tom-boy. She matched a cuteness that none of the other Neher children had. She learned easy.

The growing and harvesting seasons came and went. Since North Dakota placed as one of the semi-arid states, the Elm Creek range took its course of heat barrier as did other regions, as well as the whims of no precipitation. Long weeks of drought was the number one ordeal. Or, when a good stand of a crop was suddenly pulverized by a hailstorm, the distraught farmer would curse the calamity ... or cry in lamenting prayer. The fortunate neighbors, whose fields were spared, would judge

... often without mercy. Especially the righteous who delved on a certain one-Scripture verse. Despite the fact that most settlers adhered to the Word of God, the demon entered the course, especially in the self-righteous judging of others. There was too much of that. Ignorance, in all generations, does its damage.

There was special virtue at the end of each day. The tricks of the setting sun had great aspiration for me. No matter how tired after a long summer's day, a sudden burst of strength led me up to the play-hill, a bit northwest of the cow-fence. Here I grasped moments of ecstasy about the horizons. I watched the sunsets with great fascination mixed with a bit of alarm. The gold-rimmed clouds meeting with horizon's pinkish buttes aroused a teenager's senses to a reverential awe. But the sun's setting behind a wall of dark clouds, I knew would bring a thunderstorm for the night. I didn't like them. I trudged down the slant and heard Momee calling, asking me to set the bowls on the table, as she set a metalic pitcher that contained cow-warm milk in the center. It made a nice table picture. The table was covered with a practically new oilcloth dotted with flowers and on both sides of the pitcher, set two plates, prime full of bread-hunks. We crowded around the table, Dadee at the head, folding hands and leaning ahead, indicating fatigue. We prayed together. Then Momee had her say: "Dunken brot in die warme milch, zödlen a-a bisle zucher euvers ... essen euch satt .. dan gehner schloffa!" (Dunk the bread into the warm milk, sprinkle a little sugar in and eat yourselves full ... then go to sleep!) Which we children would do. But we kept eyeing Dadee. Momee had set a dish containing black olives before him and a piece of meat which we children did not get. Even though we, too, craved for it. A man was fed more meat and received special favors at family meals in many German homes. It was believed the fathers needed the extra nutrition and needed to be treated as the special king of the family. A medieval tradition that weighed heavily on family equality, especially the female sect.

The subject has been America's debate and woman's plight for much too long. The honoring aspect depends solely on the respect and love the head-king has for his subjects ... the wife and family. Yes, leaders we need, such that rule with integrity.

One late summer's evening seventeen milk cows were driven into the cow-fence. One was missing, Scheck. Each cow had a name and each of us girls were assigned to milk (by hand) a couple of cows, suitable to our age. Momee would not allow any of us to milk Scheck. She had a foxy nature. If a horse fly stung her, she would kick to torment's inferno. It seemed she had more of a forebearance when Momee milked her.

Scheck's milk was rich. Momee had a reason to milk her last because the yellow creamy milk was strained into a porcelain dish-pan where a couple of rennet tablets were added. By morning no better junket there was! Then Momee heated the curdled milk and poured the substance into an empty salt-sack, draining off the whey ... tied it firmly and placed it on a cloth-covered chair. Then she placed a choice prairie stone on it for a good press. No better tasting cheese was there in the whole Mercer County!

It was no wonder that Scheck's milk was the richest as she was everlastingly looking for greener pasture ... where no other cow could maneuver, Scheck did. She would jump fences and find the neighbor's most lush field or menace their outer garden. A yoke was the only solution, but for a time it had to be removed to allow a sore to be healed.

Yes, Scheck was missing. Sure enough over the hill to the Deep Creek where a smudgy mud hole was, Scheck was ... mired into the mud to the middle of her massive belly. Pitifully she gazed at us and grunted a longing moo. As we neared with the steady draft horse, Frank, and with agonizing struggle Dadee worked a rope around her belly and ordered Dilda to lead Frank for a pull. Frank snorted, gazed with a disgusted look at Scheck, then gave a hard draw and pulled her out, slimy and shivering, the fence-ripper got out of the quick-sand!

"We've got to get rid of her!" But, NO! Scheck belonged to the Prairieland's domain. Momee would take some of the delicious rennet-cheese over to Burkhardts and say: "This was made out of Scheck's milk!" "Ja, von dem narr-vieh, gooter kaez!" (Yes, from the crazy cow, good cheese!)

It's been a number of years since the Johannes Gemeinde served the German families of the area but attendance at its Sunday services diminished. The closeness of farmers caused stock to break fences and threaten crop-fields, riling up neighbors against one another. Dissension arose and the animosity tended toward an unrest in the church. Neighbors quarreled. Judging played havoc with the congregation.

One such incident clearly indicated the revolt. A German family drove by buggy through the school yard shortly after a Sunday service. The father dismounted the buggy and hastened to where a stone lay, picked it up, and threw it with all his angry fury against the west wall of the school-house, condemning the Johannes "bruder" (brethren).

A mission minister received the notice of the disorder. Never in my young life have I heard a minister shout as he did. He stood near the teacher's desk, flashing his left hand in the air for emphasis and, with the right hand holding the open Bible, most naturally to the woe-be-gone Scripture. In a loud voice he let the "bruder" have it. He called for repentance. As his admonition subsided, the flush-faced pastor called on one of the brethren to lead in a sinner's prayer. The service ended with the hymn: "So wie ich bin, vom sturme gejagt, Mit bangen Zweifeln oft geplagt, Vom feind bedroht und sehr verzagt, O Gottes Lamm, ich komm, ich komm!" (Just as I am, though tossed about; with many a conflict, many a doubt; Fightings and fears within, without: O Lamb of God, I come, I come!)

On this Sunday of censure, it was the "vorsteher's" (elder's) duty to invite the guest minister for noon eats. We gathered as a family near about the teacher's desk where Momee laid out her bakes and sausage. I see Momee slice with a roundly-worn butcher knife a huge loaf of her everlasting yeast bread. And lay out the precious "zugar-kuchen" (sugar bakes). Both Dadee and Momee acted prominent to have the preacher eat with us.

I've never, ever seen another man devour hunk after hunk of bread as this minister did ... and his stout body showed it too. In those days, to be well-rounded indicated good health ... "Der isch gut gfuehdert" (he is well-fed) was a common saying, often said with a note for good-to-look-at, as something desired. For a minister to eat heartily was a compliment to the "hausfrau" (housewife), a favorable impression. I saw Momee laugh, a kind of a characteristic chuckle, amused at this bread-hungry preacher.

The Sunday ended with an afternoon "versamlung" (prayer meeting). Evidently the last in that schoolhouse.

The timely reconciliatory sermon had little effect on the parish. Church life dwindled for another reason: the English language began to have priority and school pupils were urged to attend Sunday School at Elm Creek School #1. Mrs. Jack Crowley had the oversight there and directed the music as well as the lection lessons.

It seemed Dadee didn't mind when we girls scampered across the hills to the northeast schoolhouse for an English Sunday School afternoon-session. I was elated and very much overtaken with happy singing as Mrs. Crowley played music on a small organ. She could play and sing so beautifully that it cast a reverence in the atmosphere. It had something so ideal that it affected us children. As part in a drama that made us feel uplifted in awe, as if it was an angel singing. We've never seen nor heard the sound of an organ before. And Ruby Crowley moved this young schoolgirl with a spontaneous personal impulse so that I walked up and stood close to the organ. Completely preoccupied with the words of the hymn Mrs. Crowley sang, "When The Roll Is Called Up Yonder I'll Be There." I leaned over and laid my head on her arm. In view of the other children I didn't even imply a bit of shyness. It was a kind of a divine call ... and Mrs. Crowley abided with a tender touch! "Yes, Jesus wants children's names written on the roll!"

The Roaring Twenties
Prairie's Generosity

We enter the 'roaring twenties'! They were the generous years. As families grew and became more resourceful, two or three-story houses arose. Even out in the remote country, the prairieland sufficed and farmers/ranchers chanced to build.

Realizing the crowded conditions in our home, Dadee presented a generous suggestion at a family-meal time, that if we all work hard we could enlarge the house with an upstairs and a full cellar. Of course, we promised for a common workmanship.

Neher made a deal with Jake Neuhardt, a Hebron carpenter, that if he would direct the project, Dadee would supply the workers. The pay would be a winter's supply of meats for the Neuhardt family. Neuhardt loved Momee's 'chickie' meat ... so meat was the payment.

As was, everybody slaved. A horse-drawn scraper made the excavation of the plastic clay earth a torture, even worse than digging coal. I see Dadee bending his head to avoid striking it against the base of the old cellar as the horses tugged forcibly the excavation ... man and horses dripping with sweat. We girls lugged pailful after pailful of loose dirt up to enlarge the cellar. "Wenn mir a-a groeseres haus wellen, muszmer a-a schaffa!" (If we want a bigger house then we must work for it!) And a big house we did get!

Three bedrooms and one closet ... upstairs. One kerosene lamp that set on the only dresser in the middle room. It was all the light there was. Here is where we stuck in the curling iron for a quick curl and for a sure hair scorch ... so much that the offensive smell penetrated all over the spacious house.

To look for the right pettycoat or underwear, holding the lit-lamp in one hand, sorting the shelf's mixed up garb with the other, and shouting with mouth to a sister, baffled me yet today that the house didn't take to fire. That one kerosene lamp! What light this simple 'homestead' lamp illuminated ... a torch of enlightenment for the Neher girls.

The standards of life got better. Even in the Neher home. New, ingenious farming equipment and homemaking items came into American homes. They eased the hard, laborious part of life. They even changed attitudes. Still dependent on horse and man, except for more mechanized performance. People worked for better things as well as for style; life was becoming more bearable. The anticipation for better things in life was at hand.

Even the shiny chrome on the Majestic kitchen range added beauty to the kitchen; and with all its noted qualities, we loved the way it cooked up a storm. It was Momee's pride. A soft cloth in her apron pocket laid on a rub at any time as she worked with food. On Saturdays 'Bon Ami' did the real shine.

I see a replica of great cooking and baking in this ornate wood and cook stove ... no prior stove could match the reliable Majestic. The tea-kettle singing its steam out on a Winter's day; a kettle of 'borscht' (vegetable soup) simmering on a back lid; the removing of four huge golden brown loaves of bread and the shoving in of the second batch; the heating of three sad irons as Odeela changed about by turns, one iron after another, to iron the sprinkled-starched-wash. Shirts and dresses had to be ironed just so. Momee was proud that Odeela ironed in a particular manner.

Its reservoir, with its ever-ready warm water, proved to be a very handy utility ... for the wash basin, for the dishes, for the crubbing of the floors, etc., heated water was always available! Then there was the warming cabinet with two access doors. The adjustable damper which controlled baking temperature, situated at the base of the stove pipe which arched into the chimney. Each Spring the stove pipes would be taken down and the soot removed. Then Momee would give it a shiny black coat of stove-pipe-paint. Even a black shiny coal pail, filled with wood or coal, set in front close to the loading door. The Majestic served also to keep the kitchen warm.

Of all the north-home's appliances, I find it in my resolve that our Majestic stove has given us food and warmth, an animation to the prairie home!

"Let's have one more hunk of bread that the Majestic baked!"

To be able to attest to encounters of "firsts" in one's lifetime is a prime influence for this book. There were numerous beginnings during the 'roaring twenties' ... so much for changes that woman would cry out: "Gottes Willa! Was noch alz?" (God's will, what else yet?)

I remember, as if by a mysterious assault, the coming of a gasoline-powered vehicle, as it drove along the meandering road and roared into our yard. It frightened chickens into a frenzy ... dogs barked ferociously ... my sister and I ran behind the house in fright. Dadee had a spirited team of horses hitched to the wagon ... and Lady reared and Mike snorted! Dadee pulled the lines to control the horse act, in a sideway glance, he laughingly shouted at the rancher Keogh. The proud driver sat very erect, tightly holding the steering wheel and anchoring his feet as if to keep a hold on it. The car had two kerosene lamps in front on each side of the windshield which permitted fair lighting.

Keogh and Neher obviously dealt with their cattle-deal business, but their main jest for conversation was the car. "I cranked myself to death before it sputtered a roar," joshed Keogh. "Seems we've got to get to know one another!"

A magic monster ... a mysterious thing that runs without a horse! That's all taking place in our yard. And the man reflects a strangeness as well. This is all outside the familiar. "Liever alles!" (Dear all!)

This model had no top and no spare tire. As when a flat tire, the driver hoisted up the wheel with a jack, removed the tire and tube and fixed the puncture, gluing on a patch ... then the trudge of pumping in the air. The language would get vigorous but the will to be master of the new subject eased the drudgery.

Baggage was strapped onto the side of the running board. The irregular tank placement did not allow a free flow of gasoline to the engine, especially uphill. Then the driver would turn around and back up the hill. As when the very first car drove into our yard, it created a havoc and scare ... what an invention! Would we have believed what more was ahead?

Mr. Tigen was teacher that year. I must have been in the fifth grade. Mr. Tigen taught all eight grades, but his favorite group was the smaller children. He would become so enthused about the stories he told the children as they sat on the front class-bench, that he didn't notice what went on behind him. The upper-grade outlaws jumped out of the northeast window without the teacher becoming aware of it. Mr. Tigen's leniency in discipline became a problem. The school board issued a warning without much of a change in the general discipline-order. One day the County Superintendent appeared during morning's patriotic exercises. Tigen was so involved in a dramatic performance that he did not see the supervisor. The older kids giggled while the small ones took it all in with open mouths. Without more fanfare the elite man 'spit out', as was the social technique of the upper-class. By now Tigen had been conscious of the visitor. He bent down by the teacher's desk and pulled out a spittoon, and placed it next to the chair where the superintendent sat.

School session was dismissed. I had had taken off my shoes, among the stunts that happened that morning. As we marched outdoors, I stepped into the brownish splash of spit ... phew!

Mr. Tigen was the prototype of Ichabod Crane, riding a lanky bay mare to school ... his feet were way too long for the stirrups and his straight hair streamed backward as the horse went at a fast pace while he came pounding down the dirt road, usually a bit late.

Mr. Tigen's teaching tenure in Elm Creek School #2 did not last the term. His talent and love reigned with the younger set, but he lacked knowledge and the character to rule the older kids. 'Either you do a good job with all the grades or out you go!' (a school board quote.)

As Mr. Tigen packed his belongings, I beheld the ornate spittoon he owned. Could such a thing of beauty be used to spit into?

This was the age for "spittin'" and "spittoons" too! Whether it was the lack of vitamin C in diets or the smoke and snuff of tobacco that generated a saliva or winter's colds that caused a lot of "spittin'" is yet to be proven. But spitting any place must have been in style.

When Andrew Jackson became president in 1829, his first official act was ordering twenty new spittoons for the White House. Those were mostly made of china and were very adorned. Therefore, the spittoon became something of a 'monument' to the Capitol scene ... as well as a necessary item in any office.

In the average commoner's home, it was the slop pail, coal pail or just plain "spittin'" the stuff all over the floor. No worse loathe was there in my life. My stomach turned up to a spew just listening to the secreting ... and then for the ready aim of the spat! What a sickening effect it had on the onlooker!

Whether you belonged to a higher social or prominent set, or whatever creed or ethnic-type of a person you were, to all, the spitter was eventually considered a nasty person. Why should a cleaning maid be expected to carry and clean out offensive stuff? The ethical manners, a part of clean America, set in , and made the spittoon unacceptable and the spitter, a social vice.

It took a lot of convincing on the part of Knife River/Elm Creek locality people to believe, that it was actually true, that one neighbor could take a 'receiver' off the hook on this lifeless, rectangular-type box that hung on the wall ... hold the device to the ear and hear a neighbor talk. It was something like a ghost that uttered words and haunted fright. An indication of a supernatural voice of no good intent. "Was noch als in Amerika?" (What else yet in America?) The most recent settlers who couldn't read had it hardest to believe. I trust to believe that Matt Crowley dealt with the Telephone Company as to the charter.

Gradually though the ultimatum faced them. Even if neighbors had been stubbornly opinionated, the decision was reached to form a party-line and Hebron was to be the Central Station.

After the poles were stomped in and wires lifted and anchored on a glass insulator, which was screwed on a spiked wooden bracket ... the telephones were attached and fastened onto walls of homes, and the lines were directed to Hebron's switchboard. Here a trained operator (Central) handled the calls that were directed to a different line or town residents.

The head-family man's name was given a designated number, or call, which we called 'their ring'. You could call any neighbor, such as two, three and four shorts; or alternates with longs and shorts ... a kind of a Roman numeral system where XXI meant two long and one short ring. One long ring called the Central ... she would ask "Number, please." Then she would connect you with another line and ring the friend's number. There were no directories the first years, so we memorized the business and residential numbers. Chaos, yes!

The job of repair and upkeep was a community affair. Most line/pole damage would be caused by bad weather or lightning striking a pole, or a blast into the phone. A gadget called the 'lightning arrester' directed the bolt into the ground by way of an iron rod. A close bolt often blew the telephone off of the wall. Or, fire would occur and occasionally a home burned to the ground. All around, the mystifying telephone didn't deserve a woman's trust.

During a summer morning's breakfast, a spasmodic thunder-head flashed several severe lightning bolts ... one striking the telephone, engulfing it in flame. Dadee quickly dipped a dish towel into a basin of water, slapping the flame and calling for Hammer Soda! Thrusting the powdery soda against the spreading flame soon extinguished the fire. The catastrophy shocked Momee to hysteria. She threw her arms up and shouted, "Nimm des ding ausem haus naus!" (Take this thing out of the house!)

Well, the scare-monger phone got to be Momee's very close companion, a means to visit with friends. For emergency calls, business plans, news, meetings and plain gossip, the phone drew the isolated farm families closer together, for better or worse! If "the worse" has rated as "the worst", it would have to be the "rubber-neck" who listened to every ring and knew everybody's affairs as well as the weaknesses of everybody in the neighborhood. Despite its lack of privacy, the country telephone line-system left a significant line for the pioneer's new fangles ... a line for the heritage news!

Lately new items were added to homes as well as to the farm-yard. Curiosity, excitement and feelings of 'making-it-well' overwhelmed families. The Nehers included.

Dadee arrived home from Hebron with a double-deck wagon-load of supplies. The three horses that had been hitched to the grain-loaded wagon had something of a load to pull on the home-bound trip as well. The load included a new washing machine with a deep-wedged tub, wooden-grip handles and attached to it a hand conveyable wringer with rubber rollers. The tub, replenished with sudsy water, held a good pile of wash. It was hand-driven by one of us girls for some minutes, then piece by piece twisted into the wringer and wrung into a tub of rinse-blue water ... again re-wrung into a clothes basket for hanging out on a new washline. A sudsy water-change was necessary for a large wash such as for fifteen piles.

It was Momee's pleasure to shake out, piece by piece, and hang it on the line with hold-on clothes pins that were so handy. Never, ever before have I seen my mother smiling during wash-time as she did today. The new 'handle' machine and the teenage girls forged the power to washing and finished the wash-work in half the time. By noon the clothes were on the line. Well, Momee, so pleased with a white-wash, just soaked it all in!

At this point the yard received a magic apparatus that wheeled in the air and obeyed the wind ... the windmill! You see them rising in nearly every farm-yard. the wheel goes round and round, slow or faster, according to the breeze or according to the force of the wind. The wind energy empowers the working parts which are attached to the water pump, drawing water from the well through the pump-spout and spilling it into the stock tank. The wheel whirs so fast and towers over the prairieland ... Oh, such a fine thing!

But one day, the Neher windmill raced out of control. It could not be stopped. The rocker-arm stuck just a trifle. In no way could a big-bodied person get near the trouble-spot without being caught by the winding wheel and likely thrown out yonder for a last flight! It wasn't a hard thing to detach. "Paulie, denkscht, kannscht du gut oof-basa un des losz ziega?" (Paulie, do you think you can be very careful as you detach it?), anxiously queried Dadee. Instantly I obeyed. Quickly I climbed up and raised the rigid piece ... at minute's time I was caught by the wheel's flap and at the very moment Dadee used all his effort to shut off the windmill ... a moment's precision saved my life! However, the fleshy part of the back of my right leg received a triangular tear ... a dangle! Yes, a clear,

three-cornered mark I have yet to this day.
 The Windmill! The merry-go-round wheel ... it rose over the prairie and field plateau, augmenting a melody with rhythmic sounds created by the winds ... the water-pumping song of the hilly prairieland!

The 1918 influenza epidemic reached over the country and took thousands of lives, practically wiping out entire families in some localities. The disease crept into the Neher home as well. Several of the family members were very sick, especially Dadee. I heard him moan and alarm in fever heat. I saw Momee cry, as she injected into Dadee's fever-swollen mouth, tablespoon after tablespoon of home-brewed whiskey, which a neighbor had brought over. The orders spread that whiskey or wine was the ultimate medication. And so true it was. It saved Dadee's life.

Dadee made it a clear-cut anecdote in general conversation that whiskey is good for anything that ails one. Guess what Dadee's project got to be? He set up a whiskey brewing apparatus in the summer-kitchen. In a corner set a 20-gallon crock containing a fermenting-rye-substance. Close to the ceiling entwined the narrow pipes ... one end sucking in the steam from the boiler which contained the ready brew. I see Dadee push in the stove a dry cob so to keep a slow fire for an even temperature that was just right for a steady steam. On the other end of the pipe dripped out the precious droplets of whiskey. Therefore Dadee had whiskey on hand, whether you were well or whether you were sick!

I refuse to comment on the Prohibition Law!

Clara, the baby and eighth of the Neher children, was born on Aug. 19, 1922. She was delivered by Mother Lennick and assisted by Mother Burkhardt. That day we were shocking grain bundles after a bountiful crop. "Schon wieder a-a baebe!" (Again, another baby!) The baby cried a lot and seemed to be sickly. Her navel was bound tightly with a long strip of cloth. The baby existed in pure agony. The abdomen cramped. All the 'brauching' (spiritual meditating) didn't soothe a hurting infant. This was just one of the baby-care myths that was passed down which caused undue suffering for the newborn!

The Autumn moons during the Roaring Twenties held strong memories of the Elm Creek schools. We had our initial brush with education. The big, brown, frame schoolhouse, headed by both male and female teachers, remains a silent testament to traditions and values of our immigrant-settlers ... which was made up of a combined heritage of different nationalities.

This was a typical American country school ... in work and play alike, where we spoke English and where the children were taught to conform to American ways. Learning English and being patriotic were vital steps in the Americanization process. At this point immigrant parents were willing to let their children take the step but they did not want them to lose the native tongue, the German background families especially. Rightfully speaking, it did cause problems.

Elm Creek schools experienced discrepancy, which crept from neighbors' disputes and school board charges. And the overgrown pupils got to be harder and harder to keep in orderly control. The teacher, as was the general rule to discipline, used abusive measures ... such as hitting with a stick, belt or whip. Definitely wrong psychology was used, especially for the sensitive children.

I'm reminded of an episode in the life on one pupil, Martha Martin, who could not memorize the multiplication tables and for each wrong number she was hit on her clenched finger-tips with a stick by this ferocious teacher. An older brother, Fred, intercepted the cruel beat and handed the teacher a fist's blow to the chin. Martha's fingers bled and the teacher's tongue stained her hand and dress with dripping blood.

School was dismissed. In fact for days. Nevertheless, the same teacher returned, determined to use her tyrannical power to discipline. It was a frightful lot of kids. Except for the older pupils. They resisted the rebel teacher. One older pupil expressed her inner feelings on a piece of paper. The note reached the teacher alright, thus arousing an immediate commotion. The doomed school kids were denied their noon hour. The irate teacher, in brazen line, wrote the script on the blackboard: "Teacher is a ass-hole!" There was snickering among the older boys ... otherwise, a loathsome stillness! Every pupil was handed the chalk and had to write her/his art of handwriting as the note read ... for similar match of identity. Teacher took notes. It got to be tiresome ... until all the Boehlers, Burkhardts, Crowleys, Martins, Schnaidts were through, I, a Neher, was hungry and bored ... a close last one to be called. All of us skeptical pupils had had a chance to study the foul statement. But when my turn came I let the teacher know that "a ass-hole" was wrong ... it should be "an ass-hole!" "Will you shut up and go back to your seat!" she flared.

The verdict, truly said, was irrational. Evelyn Boehler and Emelia Martin were chosen as the outlaws ... their penmanship matched closest to the critical comment. Each received a beating. The rest of us were ordered to remain seated but a couple of the older boys attacked the teacher, so to end the abusive act.

However, that wasn't the end of things. As usual the teacher returned to school the next morning. The majority of the dire-minded kids were about the school-yard. Several of the older boys were missing. The school-bell rang and we all proceeded to our seats. There appeared an odor, suggestive of something. The teacher sat down by the teacher's desk and in her invariable manner, opened the top drawer to fetch her rule-stick, when "fie-ew!" Human dung covered the teacher's precious items as well as the rule-stick! The teacher screamed and the pupils fled to the homes.

Rebellion? Of course! The bigger boys had to take over and rid Elm Creek School #2 of its menacer ... for the tongue-divided school board members failed to recognize the teacher's harmful influence on the pupiils. Out of the scum of things, there always something sings! A man-teacher, who needed no rule-stick, took over and Americanized, to a degree, the Elm Creek region.

The 'roaring-20's' era marks the height of country-school's resourcefulness. Not only in North Dakota, but in all Plains States. The school functions created a niche among the different nationality-settlers. It was the time when families, as a whole, took part. Schools were better furnished, better lit and more comfortable. The fuller book shelves became a source of a desire for learning for both young and old.

The Elm Creek schools were used as part of Winter's gatherings. Spelling bees, arithmetic contests and debates were held in school. Socials, picnics, elections. In school #2 dancing activities were prohibited. Meetings of all sorts became popular and were held in schoolhouses. Occasionally a brave teacher would board there despite the coyote howls.

The two major activities that drew people together were school programs and basket socials. We grew up with the schoolhouse as the center of our lives. Here is where not only sad things happened, the fun thing-in-itself, remains a fundamental truth that laughter in those days outweighed the gravenesses of our lives. We learned to laugh despite our harassment of disturbing experiences. Playing jokes on one-another gave rise to laughter ... such as, placing a special package under the school's Christmas tree for a gift-hungry hired man ... one of Matt Crowley's ranch hands. He opened it quickly, after Santa Claus had handed it to him and found three swine-tails neatly wrapped in red crepe paper. And the poor guy's face turned as red as the crepe paper. Then in return, the same hired man would bid up on a certain girl's basket at a basket social, so to make the 'darn fool' pay for his girl's basket. All for restitution on the fool-proof 'pig-tails' gift ... so also to make the tricks the bud for laughter.

Holiday programs filled the schoolhouses with capacity audiences. Young and old came from far distances and squeezed into every nook, especially for the Christmas program ... with its Nativity scene, dialogues, recitations and carols. Pupils readying themselves behind black curtains and excitedly speaking or acting out their parts, entertained and educated the audience.

Oh, for those old-fashioned Christmas programs!

Elm Creek schools occasionally presented Halloween, Thanksgiving and Valentine's Day programs as well. I remember one patriotic program especially where we honored our soldiers who fought for this great country. I recited, with great emphasis, the famous "In Flander's Fields".

Mr. Dick Salmon taught School #1 and Mrs. Salmon, our school. They planned a Valentine's Day program to be presented at Mr. Salmon's school. The program numbers included pupils from both schools. Pauline Neher was selected to do a romantic dance skit with Stanley Smith. Polly (as Mrs. Salmon called me) was teased to near distraction by the school kids. Inferior feelings arose. To dance with Stanley Smith? The privilege of riding on a horse-driven sleigh to Mrs. Salmon's home and eat supper with the celebrity-family was enough initiation for a hay-seed. I felt like chaff.

It was a beautiful moon-lit February evening as the Salmons and Polly were sleigh-racing to the team's trot over the snow-swept road to the Smith ranch. "Come on, Polly, let's get into the Smith home where it's warm," soothed Mrs. Salmon ... as the man-teacher unhitched the horses. What an elaborate parlor! There hung a Coleman light from the ceiling. A couch and some stuffed animals hung on the walls which the Smith's must have hunted down. And near at hand set a Morning Glory phonograph! The kindly little lady, Mrs. Smith, affectionately tried to make me feel comfortable. But I felt strangely out of place. All in all, this was too much!

It was time to practice the skit. Here comes Stanley walking into the parlor, ready to dance with the fair little stranger. He didn't look like any of our school's boys ... he was tall, and his expression, so serious and explicit. Mr. Salmon wound up the phonograph and out blared the waltz-like music! Mrs. Salmon guided my steps and Mr. Salmon helped Stanley to get the drift. As for the refrain we were to hold hands for a turn-about swing. We got through it ... but my inner spirits blew it! The teasing at school and the admonition at home, that dancing was sinful, played havoc with my reactions. Frightened as all-out, I lurked out of the house. I ran to the sled and crawled under the robe for cover from the frigid coldness. The distraught dancer was found ... the skit went on, but Stanley had a different partner. However, out of the 'condemned' Polly arose a 'confident' Pauline who vibrated into dancing waltz-like notes where no sinful notes are sounded!

Valentine's Day observations took on new flair during the 1920's. During Miss Prill's short teaching tenure at our school, the Valentine box received special trimming ... a glorious red and white crepe paper, trimmed with a lace-like band and a rainbow colored bow on top resulted in the fanciest display. The petite teacher introduced a touch of luxury and color into the school. And that of exchanging names created exclamations, such as "That's telling!"; "How about that! I got her name!"; "Who'd you get, Ferdinand?"; "Don't be silly!"; "Quit asking questions!"; "I won't keep this name," injected Vera, "I hate him!" as she howled with laughter.

Of course Miss Prill received the most Valentines. She was particularly excited about one special fancy Valentine! You see, Miss Prill fell foolishly in love with one of her teenage pupils, Albert Martin; then one of the mischievous older boys signed Albert's name to a love-message Valentine. It seemed like an uncontrollable seizure that contained Miss Prill when she discovered the intent Albert had. Henceforth, during recesses, she would chase her imaginary boy-friend, placing undue emotional strain on the poor innocent lad who couldn't have been more naive about the whole situation.

Soon afterward the distraught little teacher, along with disciplinary problems, began being absent, leaving school kids at random. The final doctor's diagnosis appeared to be that she remain in bed to regain the strength of her nerves. In short, a nervous breakdown! Poor Miss Prill had to be ordered to board the east-bound train where her kind of weaker people lived. To cope with School #2, where the offspring were that of Prairieland's tough makings, required a tougher teacher.

    The country schoolhouse era belongs to a very special period of time by distinctive character. It turned out quality students who went on to higher education or settled on variant occupations.
    The 'roaring-20's' years of Elm Creek schools set its merited worth. No former or later era matched its quality. It turned out distinguished and useful citizens who we call the Prairieland's first generation. Its pupils, despite their harrowing experiences, learned the fundamentals of life ... especially that of work. They received a source of knowledge that broadened their views and they learned that nationality differences added to the resourcefulness of a new America. Its pupils had much to offer in turning out to be creative citizens who could share with one another and who found their niches in life.
    The Elm Creek/Knife River's pioneer children became a 'melting pot' of various professional, vocational and agricultural type people ... standing out in such occupations as homemakers, farmers, ranchers, mechanics, salesmen, businessmen and women, office personnel, clerks, cafeteria workers, seamstresses, shoe repairmen, gardeners, nurses, teachers, clergy, college instructors, pilots, newspaper employees and an author.
    Those who were called to serve our country abided in military service in demanding areas, and served with integrity and honor. Hail to country-school pupils!

Among the teachers who taught at the big, brown schoolhouse during the years I attended country-school were Mr. Salmon, Mr. Tigen, Miss Steinkraus, Miss Doherty, Miss Prill, Mrs. Salmon and Miss Ball. Miss Bacon, Mr. Anderson and others followed. Every teacher left a significant impression on a pupil's character. As well as lessons learned that remained resolute throughout life. Mrs. Salmon stressed body and mouth cleanliness. Brushing teeth and washing the tongue, reaching way back, probably is the reason I still have my own teeth and haven't had much trouble with bad breath.

Oh, for those schoolmarms! But not quite as preferred as man-teachers for a country school ... naturally tradition had it that a man had a better sway of the school bell!

Bums and horse thieves were a threat in those days. The bums, riding the train's freight cars, then jumped off by smaller towns, then fumbled around the streets, looking for something to eat. Naturally the sheriff would shoo them out of town. Invariably they'd wander along the prairie roads and end up at a farm home ... hungry, thirsty and dirty. With children scampering about, the bum-pair would befriend the curious little ones, while the neighbor's wife was in the house, praying. It was her holy duty to feed them, but her inner nature rebelled: "Go and work!" she shouted. "Who doesn't work shall not eat!" Even so, she fed them, and , commanding them to leave, or she'd sic the dog after them. Leave they did with no remorse.

A lone cowboy, riding about, over hill and vale, was on the whole, welcome. As he led his pony to the water-tank he swished his sweaty head and face in a blow and wash. Farm families knew he was a friend. A cowboy was a common guest at our house.

Occasionally a posse of elite riders rode across the country, pack and gun attached to the saddle and managing their ponies at a swift pace. These were the dangerous ones, and could be spotted in a hurry. What an image against a sunset as they rode along the slanting hills!

Living close to the Crowley ranch and being distant neighbors to the Schaeffner ranch, the Neher place rendered itself as an appropriate overnight stay for three horse bandits. I've never seen Dadee so scared. They made themselves at home by the haystack premises. The horses' snoots were burrowed into the stack for fresh oats hay. Of course they asked for bread ... and as Dadee handed it to them, they warned against any reporting. What a frightful and vigilant night it was!

At daybreak they mounted their ponies and headed north, snipping every fence. They were out to steal a few prime horses. This was their business ... they acted their course with no remorse!

Rumors were that there was one killing ... a

man! Whether it was a ranch-hand or one of the bandits, we'll never know. For he was buried near the spot where he was shot. Investigation? "Hell-no," remarked an old-timer, "that was the game of the time!"

The Prairieland echoes Autumn time! The air is getting nippy and the wild geese are flying in a perfect "V", southbound.

At nearly every Autumn of my septuagenarian life I hiked the prairies. I waited for a sky-croon, that of a goose-call ... a kind of a sound that beckons one out to Elm Creek country. We walk the hills and recall the happy treads of childhood and the teenage responsibilities of prairieland's domain.

Every sign bids farewell to the previous season. We sense an atmosphere of change ... a transformation of a growing period to fruition.

Prairieland's bounty. We find the fiery red rose-hip berries so delicious and nutritious. The bulberry, clusters of red berries hanging on to provide feed for the winter bird and a season's appetizer for the hiker. In an inconspicuous hole near a bush by a field where the country-mouse has stored her winter's feed, we smile at animal's instinctive habits. We see a rabbit jumping out of its familiar nest from under a sagebrush that matches its fur. It scampers along a meandering trail about the hill, not too afraid.

We hiked on and saw the "No Hunting" sign attached to a gate-post. It is all for the good of preserving Nature's creatures and its natural environment. Man has already ruined too much. There's something sacred about Prairieland's wildness!

It happened during the 'roarin' twenties'! The English language became a priority in our home. It all happened so naively. The teacher, Miss Bacon, who boarded at our home, had much to do with it. Very casually she instructed us older girls not to call each other those German-addicted names: Dilda we should call Matilda; Odeela, Tillie; Paulie, Pauline; Elza, Elsie; 'der boi', Edwin ... as for Anna and Clara, they always had the American sound. "And get away from those pet names, Dadee and Momee, for your parents," she urged. "Call them plain Pa and Ma!"

Although our German dialect remained intact, America's English language echoed a more fitting tone in the Neher home. And it seemed Pa's interests Americanized as well.

Over the hill and down the road clanked a black, illustrious tractor that replaced the steam engine, creating a scene that was hard to believe. A mechanized crawler that was empowered by gasoline, pulled the massive thresh-machine to an adjoining field near the yard. A new, efficient machine that tractor was!

The field was filled with shocks which we girls had shocked. The straw-pile was to be close to the yard for convenient winter feeding. The thresher was placed in accordance and the tractor unhooked and set at a distance. The massive belt was unwound from its framework and drawn on the flywheels of tractor and separator. These were emotional times! You see, Pa was tractor-man and Uncle Fred Martin, separator-man, and each hated to have the other boss him. Smart slams were thrown at each other ... in German, of course! The brothers-in-law feuds were quite common.

The tractor was spurting its roar to an energetic and steady pitch bringing the separator to a deep-set whir. What commotion! Is everything going to work? Bring in the first load!

Two wagons, their racks piled high with grain bundles, drew close to the hungry mouth of the great machine. The teams of horses had to be trained and conditioned to the noise. Two Martin boys threw into the canvas conveyor the grain bundles, the head part first. Then into the maw, the slashing teeth devoured the bundles ... a puff of dust, the chaff shot from the mouth of the pipe and started a pile on the ground. On the other side the first bushel of golden grain flowed from the chute into the wagon. Here is where my job was ... to level the grain on the wagon-box as well as help Pa cast shovelful after shovelful into the granary. Of the Martin young people, the boys that were still home, George, Henry and Albert, their sister Martha and my sisters Matilda and Tillie, were the regular bundle haulers. Usually one of the Martin boys stayed the night so as to rise at dawn-break to help Pa feed, harness and hitch the horses. There were the twenty cows to be milked by hand, both morning and evening. Elsie managed the yardwork and Louise was Ma's helper, preparing the scrumptious lunches and meals. Both our Mother and Aunt Sophie turned out bread and kuchen bakes, which were made from everlasing yeast that mellowed with flavor and goodness.

I queried my cousin Martha whether pitching bundles is being remembered as tortuous work during her maidenly years: "I worked hard at any field work," related Martha. "You name it and I did it!" Pitching and hauling bundles was perhaps the most exhausting, as Matilda and Tillie will attest to, but we had fun too. Once we killed a snake and slung it on the hayrack lath right under the harness lines. As George 'giddy-yapped' the horses to go, snatching the lines, his foolproof nature succumbed. A snake hanging there! "I'll get even with you two," yapped George. Even the old separator and tractor men took time for a laugh!

And George did pay back the roguish tricksters ... in fact on the same day. As the thresh-crew sat around the laden dinner table, Martha and Tillie were missing. "Oh, they were sitting in the back-house paging through the Sears Roebuck catalogue," quipped George, with a silly get-on laugh. George had pushed a lath into the outside door of the out-house. Only after a "sitting-out-a-crime-time" did he release the hungry twosome!

So many tales were being told about the back-house, out-house or odd-house ... certainly it was the center of interesting doings.

The place of rest and forbearance ... Oh, what a retreat! Away from dishwashing or scrubbing, where one could sit and close one's eyes to dream; or, to listen to the droning of a few large, black flies; or, paging through the Savage catalogue ... wish upon a wish --- far too many, for all ended with a sigh. "Get out and let me in," hollered Anne, with a mingle of reprove or approve. 'Twas all in an outlandish manner that we took turns at the two-holer. You couldn't flush like the modern toilet; and neither did we have a spray freshener. You tolerated the smell because it was Nature's way. We did not mind germs because we knew not what they were.

Wintertime cast a different setting. The visitors wasted no time at the biffy-stall; we see little drifts of snow that the north wind blew through the cracks in the wall --- how well we know ... it's Nature's cleanser!

For us prairieland folk we feel an ache in our heart --- like the loss of a friend ... of the out-house, up a-ways, that came to an end!

Sod or stone barns were markers of the prairie, the kind the homesteaders built as stock shelters ... very few remnants are left. Heritage societies urge or advocate a plan to preserve what is left. In it we see rugged culture.

The second barn, built during the 1920's, stood huge in size and was used to store hay for winter; or, when empty, fiddlers or accordian players provided waltz and polka music for the merrymakers. Traveling across the country you still find an occasional well-kept, red, red barn with its ventilator-dome atop, the imaginary echo of many a story. Such as the waltzing couple tying the marriage knot and starting the prairie life where their homesteading parents left off.

Another Autumn activity that the big barn was noted for were the Husking Bee parties. Following threshing the corn had to be husked, thrown into a wagon and hauled onto a pile in a side shed. It was hard work, but the anticipation for the fun-time of a husking bee eased the task. The neighborhood young people were invited for an evening and we would all sit on the floor, Indian-style ... boys on one side and girls on the other. We would start husking and whoever found a red cob, that he/she had a choice of kissing his/her favorite gal or guy ... here is where an occasional romance sprouted. The neighbor boy married his neighbor girl. The case of either one having had one and only one match experience ... probably not much more than a friendship encounter ... yet they were married, whether the course was for better or worse, they stuck! Worse yet, when the neighbor 'dumm-kopf' (blockhead) married his cousin and then produced offspring that were 'dummer wie sie senn' (dumber than they are) ... the probable degenerating mental condition would result which would be a dilemma for their children. Relative marriages were all too common in those days!

The barn dances, that drew young people from far and near together, naturally attracted ... as when a dancing-couple held hands assisting each other down the barn ladder, then went on a moon-lit stroll. The word was said as they embraced and kissed on the wooden bridge. And the smiling moon shone down with a shine of approval for a resourceful and ethnic-mixed marriage ... a culture enhancement for America! Oh, for that romantic MOON of long ago!

Indian Summer is a period of warm and mild weather late in the Autumn season. It comes while the leaves are turning color and falling from the trees. Indian Summer has no definite date to begin or end. It is a beautiful part of Fall. It usually follows the thrust of cold weather ... often a snowfall.

The sky turns a rich blue and looks hazy near the horizons and appears and feels gentle. The Autumn colors are bidding farewell and in it is a kind of 'respect' for Nature that tells us it has supplied us with produce and now it is time for sleep. It is a kind of 'Good Earth romance' as the moon peeks through fleeting clouds on a moonlit stream.

The American Indian thoroughly enjoyed over the generations this season which was named in their honor. They called it a special gift from a favorite god – Cautantowit, which means the god of the southwest winds. The American settlers named Autumn's melodrama after the American Indian who told many stories as if from omens.

The immigrant settlers feared for a revolt of the Indians during the Indian Summer period. It was the time that the war-like Indians used their chance to prepare for more attacks on the white man. The settlers also believed that the smokiness or haze at the horizons came from fires that the Indians built on the prairies.

And how true for fearing Autumn's arrival! On Nov. 15, 1892, telegraph messages were sent to all small towns in North Dakota that the Indians had broken out of the reservation and everybody should hasten to defend themselves against attack. Rumors had been coming to Hebron as well. It was decided by the men in town to build a fortification against a possible attack. Here is were Fort Sauerkraut originated and remains as a grim testimonial of the days of the Indian scare. Stories of other uprisings usually occurred in the Fall, for the Indian needed winter food.

Again and again the Indian Summer reveals its warmth and might. The romance of our frontier days are gone for many moons, although the horizons of butte and hill hazes forevermore! Indian Summers will always be!

Saturdays on the north farm could be termed as clean-up days ... in the house as well as in the barns. Cow sheds, horse stalls and the chicken-coop. The manure had to be pitched with a specific manure-fork onto a wagon which the old team, Jack and Frank, pulled in and out and then on to the manure pile. The loading and unloading two of us girls had to do. Likewise another two girls had to do the cleaning in the house. Feuds? Of course! There's always been moaning or scolding as one or the other schemed to get out of the messy work. We did get into each other's hair since Tillie stood by the mirror and pushed a deep ridge and formed a spit-curl in her natural wavy hair, taking her time as no one else could. She had looks too and she knew it. She retained the dressing up habit all her life ... which was an asset that displayed class. Tillie was very much like Ma, meticulous with a love for the nice things, especially dresswear.

Ma was unduly fussy about the home as well as the washing, cooking and baking. On Saturdays I see her do a large batch of kuchens and kolaches and while the kitchen range was fired up, she cooked the meats, parboiled potatoes and prepared the sweet-sour cabbage dish, all for Sunday evening meals ... just in case of company. Ma was a good cook and she passed that ability on to her daughters ... to this day the old-time dishes have a way with the Neher girls.

As for the weekly house-cleaning, all beddings were changed, the wicks of the kerosene lamps were trimmed and lamp vessels filled with kerosene and the glass-globes shined. The floors, which were either varnished or painted to a bright orange, needed to be scrubbed from one end of the house to the other. The shiny parts of the heater and kitchen range couldn't show streaks.

Oh, for that vinegar jug! We added vinegar to shine the chrome, to scrub the floors, to rinse hair, to add taste to cookery, to mix with goose fat for a smear and sweat when sick. And, Oh, for the kerosene can! For burning oil of lanterns and lamps, a cleanser for a tough stain; a bug and insect repellent; for spraying the chicken coop for the lice, delousing a dog, and to massage a kid's head that had the start of lice; to sprinkle on wood for to start a quick fire in the stove. What a yelp when the can was found empty!

Butchering Days! They seemed like 'gala' affairs ... in that it involved neighbors' help making it a social activity where lots of hands helped and lots of mouths bellowed and laughed.

Watching the prairie roads for a buggy or sled to come over the hill, telling us that neighbors are coming, created an excitement. Hardly had the first neighbor unhitched his team, there jolted into the yard another family coming in a lumber wagon.

Big boilers of water were steaming and butcher knives had been sharpened the day before; as were tables, washtubs and kettles scoured and the old summer kitchen cleaned and warmed up, ever so converted to the big task of butchering. It meant getting up at 4:00 a.m.!

After an early breakfast Pa took the sharpest, long-bladed knife for the butchering act of each hog. To hold down the hog and stick the pointed knife into its lower neck, Pa aimed at the right mark to reach the heart for a quick maneuver, causing the heart to gush out the blood in quick order. A dish-pan was held close to catch the fresh, red blood for blood sausage. This scene was the most gruesome. I never did eat blood sausage. Let the allspice seasoning be right. I didn't want it!

Then followed the scalding. It took several men to dip and roll the carcass in a barrel that contained boiling hot water. Picking off and scraping the hog-hair to a cleanly effect and last rinse, one by one the lard-hogs were strung up in the barn entrance. Buckets-ful of loins, head and organs would be washed, then thrown into a boiler and simmered just right. These became delicacies, as that of head cheese, liver sausage, pickled tongue, etc. The animal's intestines were cleaned, scraped and soaked in water. A special board was used just for scraping the casings. They were used to make sausage with.

Butchering day meals were simple. The oil cloth was taken off the table and a huge kettle of homemade noodle soup, bread and kuchen set in the center and everybody reached for helpings. The second day's dinner was bound to be 'momelech soop' (a corn-meal mush swimming in a half-fat broth). I hated it, and I would heave after swallowing the first tablespoonful. "Eat it," ordered Pa. "It's good for greasing your inside!" Not very often Ma cooked something my stomach couldn't digest, but this stuff I puked out!

There had to be a smoke house at every farm ... the symbol for delicious meats. Pa knew exactly what woods to use for a smoke that savored the sausages and hams to a delicacy that could not be matched. He had a special knack for seasoning sausage and head cheese mixes ... a taste of garlic and hickory salt that stimulated an appetite. Ma would render the lard to a white delicate consistency and pour it into a 20-gallon crock. In another vessel she'd press in layers of sausages and pour over hot lard. For next summer's special company meal Ma would dig out the tasty sausage and serve it with all its freshly-made flavor. The hot lard preserver can ne'er lose its pioneer savor. One's mouth waters just thinking about the home-butchered meats that received the particular touch.

Gone are the days when butchering was a family deal; when the smoke house was never locked and when the whiff of smoke house aroma spread over hill and vale.

"Go, put in a bit of sand and a little water into the baby's bottle and shake it well," summoned Ma. "It will remove all impurities." Yes, the prairie sand cleansed baby Clara's bottle but prairie's plants played havoc with the child's health. She gasped for air. And all the more Ma closed the blanket cover to keep the child from breathing in the "giftiche luft" (poisonous air) ... an erroneous theory that was passed down from generation to generation. Allergic to pollens yet a need for oxygen! Clara's survival was a miracle.

When sickness struck, young or old, the patient was shooed to bed. Then you sank into the bed, not on it. A feather-bed was for the sick. An enormous double bed tick, topped with two massive goose-down pillows gently submerged the ailing one. In no way was there much pity exploited on the sick kid ... the soft feather bed was the comforter.

The mother would say: "Get to bed! Let's give you a good goose-fat-vinegar smear; then drink a cup of hot herb tea and cover up well for a good sweat!" This kind of treatment was used for any and all kinds of ailments.

To be sure, there were other home remedies ... in each community a bit different. To summon a doctor was rare.

A croupy child called for a goose-grease rub with a woolen sock tied around his or her neck. For the older children the smear mixture contained a few drops of turpentine. Or, the mustard plaster came into use. A sprained ankle was relieved by soaking it in an epsom salt, hot water bath; or, for a dislocated bone, you were bound to have a neighbor man practice on you. If you had a toothache you'd play a horse game with Papa! He'd tie a store string around the rotten tooth for a bridle-pretend and giddy-yap the horsie for a sudden jerk ... out would come the tooth and you'd cry and spit blood! Though only for awhile!

Little was known about germs in those days ... least of all did the lay people believe in the disease-producing germs. School teachers tried their best to teach their pupils about the contagion of germs. I recall vividly when Mrs. Salmon cancelled class periods and emphatically explained what the spread of contagious disease sicknesses can do to families. She touched on measles, mumps, scarlet fever, typhoid fever, flu. "When you notice that a horse is sick, stay away," she urged, "for you might catch the horse sickness and die even as the horse dies!" Mrs. Salmon was also conscious of the colds' spread.

But this particular Spring day Mrs. Salmon acted frightened. The second funeral caravan passed the school-house aiming for the cemetery. Black diphtheria had spread into the Fred Boehler home. Within ten days one girl and two boys (Leah, Albert and Herbert) died of this dread disease. "Oh, how terribly sick all ten of us children were," recalled Evelyn Boehler Beck, as she related the story, "and

Mother was pregnant with her eleventh child. I remember I was the first one down and the Mutter Lennick spent a lot of time at our sick-laden home trying to nurse us with her kind of remedies. She made a solution of salt and hammer-soda, with this she washed out our mouths trying hard to open a passage-way for breathing. Today I say this treatment saved the rest of us."

"The Hebron doctor, Dr. Radl, made several trips to our home but the medicine he carried in his satchel didn't do as much good as Mutter Lennick's brine. The doctor posted a 'quarantine' on our door ... we didn't know what it meant," sighed Mrs. Beck. "Mr. Lennick and his boys made the three wooden coffins and Mutter Lennick lined them with shiny white cloth. The rest of us children were so fascinated to see our dear dead ones lying in such angel-white coffins, but we did not want the Lennick boys to place the closed coffins on a wagon and then drive away. We wanted to keep them at home; they might awaken again!" lamented Mrs. Beck. "The eleventh child was born in November, 1926, and our Pa insisted we name him Herbert, after the last child who died." And Herbert Boehler II stood there listening to the heart-felt story his oldest sister told.

The minister of the German Congregational Church of Hebron, ND, the Rev. A. Schiller, performed simple outdoor and cemetery services. Well, when the third funeral was held I sat snug on a stone close to the cemetery premises, listening and watching as the minister, at grave-site rites, uttered these words: "Gottes Gnade und Hilfe sei mit euch!" (God's grace and help be with you!)

Then came the final and impressionable scene ... while the grave for the third child was being closed, Father Boehler fell to his knees, bending over the second grave-mound, crying and calling to God: "O Gott, des isch doch net dei willa!" (O, God, this can't be Your will!) God heard the bereaved father's cry ... He used man as instruments in medical research to discover the Schick vaccine which brought an end to this dreaded disease called 'diphtheria'!

Yes, empathy enters here as we witness the sunken graves of the abandoned cemeteries ... just keeping them in orderly upkeep is due and holy respect.

An abandoned little cemetery lay suppressed between two stony hills in an east/west direction. Here lie buried well over twenty pioneer's all-age children. They who laid down their lives in the pursuit and purview of Prairieland's generosity ... that the generation's children might have a better and safer way of life.

One-fourth mile to a southeast trend from the cemetery are the signs of excavation where the sod-shelters stood on the Neher homestead.

The surrounding country in all directions includes the episodes of "The Prairie Was Home!" ... the dramatic story of our fore-parents who settled on the wild and undeveloped country. They who coped with the unknown; they who trudged and labored mercilessly; they who cursed and used the prairie stone ... yet trusted Prairieland's Creator to make the hills resourceful for their survival and their children's welfare. Need we not do more than just remember?

The pathetic condition of a forsaken cemetery, eighteen miles north of Hebron, ND right by a country road, was viewed with a sigh of neglect by many a by-passer.

The story is told, as the county grader hit the remnants of a grave, he stopped instantly. It was against his conscience to grade where the dead were buried. "This hurts," remarked one of the Boehler relatives who have grandparents, a sister, three brothers and a cousin lying there. "Whether it was the remains of one of our loved ones or another that got graded up is unimportant ... but it's important that we do something to bring that little cemetery into a respectable condition."

And something was done. In the early 1980's, a crew of north-country descendants organized on an improvement project, working at it at random. We make at least one annual picnic-project ... and what reminiscences!

Oh, that the coming generation will halt for a moment of silence as you stand by the Homestead Cemetery, that which represents the many other prairie plots and sole burials. Pick a weed and sow the seed for a "labor of love and empathy."

It happened on a fiercely cold February day, probably in the early 1920's. There seemed like an atmospheric power that was different than ordinarily. Human beings and animals were touched with a kind of spasmodic pressure. The barn animals were jittery and nervous. Pa was extremely high strung. When Lady and Mike were hitched to the sled for driving to school, Lady kicked, snorted and pawed and Mike followed suit. Finally Pa, in a decisive manner, shouted the order that the young ones should stay home and we three oldest, Matilda, Ottilia and Pauline --- walk to school. We hurried off in a fast pace.

As we reached the school-hill we saw that the chimney of the school-house had broken down ... it was a shocking view. The stove pipes had been shaken, partially hanging down and one pipe lay on the floor with soot scattered all over. And the room was filled with smoke.

Mr. Salmon scolded: "Why didn't you stay home?" Only two Burkhardt boys and three Nehers were there. Mr. Salmon ordered the boys to accompany us at least to the last hill. We were next to freezing. I got numb and had to be dragged the last stretch.

We heard roars and cracks to a frightening degree. The cracking sounds rapidly repeated and the boom centered to the north. As we arrived home we were all crying from fright.

The earthquake had damaged Pa's whiskey-brewing apparatus in the summer kitchen. The winding pipes were shattered and broken, stove pipes dislodged and the roof-chimney had severed and brick were rolling down. The windmill slanted and Pa and Ma were frantic.

As we think of that ominous February morning, in lieu of Nature's outbursts even out on the rugged prairieland, we realized the natural power of God's ordinances. And that He is the ruler of all the Earth!

Breaking work-horses to riding definitely was one of my daring hobbies. I loved horses and felt close enough to every horse in the barn to assume their trust. Pet the cow-gathering was my buddy and understood my every move.

One Sunday afternoon, with Pa and Ma gone visiting, I felt a strange desire to mount Mike who had never been broken to riding. Lady and Mike, a harnessed team, had yielded to a horses' doze. I gently stroked Mike, grabbed a hold of the harness and pulled myself atop. Instantly Mike got aroused and started bucking, throwing me to a side slant into an empty stall. My older sisters heard the heavy thud ... they found me lying near the manger, unconscious. Lugging the lifeless Paulie over to the summer kitchen, they laid me near the stove, thinking the warmth would revive me.

In the meantime Pa and Ma returned home. As I regained consciousness, Ma was sobbing and dabbing warm water on my forehead and Pa was shouting at poor Matilda and Ottilia. A two-fold story resulted. No, it wasn't their fault!

Here's for another risky venture on a harnessed horse! After unhitching the five-horses from the gang plow, Ed Fischer, a hired man, challenged me to ride Jossie the leader horse, to home. It was a two-mile horseback riding chase. I hung on for dear-life, grasping the collar-sticks. My legs were intertwined into the harness. The hardest part was the down-hill speed, where, at one moment I almost lost my grip. As Jossie galloped into the yard, she raced past very close to the barn corner, then down to the water-tank, stopping suddenly and shaking the sweat-drips in a gullible snort. Ma screamed; chickens rampaged and dogs barked. I was a shaking piece of human gusto ... a miracle I'm still alive!

Each of our horses had a name and a personality. So did our cows. But Jossie, the horse, was distinctive; she was a leader, swift and beautiful as a swan. Not a kicking horse, but whatever she was hitched to, there was a good measure of pace. Her buff-brown skin shone and the white diamond mark on her forehead signified horse-class. A prairieland trotter Jossie was!

During the early 1920's, the barn was enlarged and painted a barn-red. The hayloft was packed with prairie-hay which was tossed by pitchfork onto the hay-rack and hauled near the west-front. Then pitched up into the upper door awaiting removal to the back for a good storage. It took all the energy of us girls as well as Pa's sweat of brow to fill the lofty upstairs. The haymow extended near to the open hole where the hay was pushed down into the manger.

The main divisions of the barn included the horse-stalls, the milk-cow shed, the calf stall, a feed-grinding nook, a chicken pen, and a combination of a machine shop and the car shelter where Pa housed our first Model T Ford.

The barn unit required a lot of hard work, like grinding feed and carrying pailful after pailful into a bin; manuring every stable or shed and hauling the stuff away, everything done by pitchfork; and milking the cows and harnessing the horses, watering and feeding the animals, as well as the many details that make for barn work.

Moreover, the barn was also a retreat: where the kitten was fondled and fed; where dog wagged his tail and befriended animals; where pigeons nestled in rifts and cooed their young amorously; where a hen hatched little fluffy chicks in a hidden corner nest; where cow-warm milk was squirt into a tin cup and you drank it to soothe the thirst; where you curried the horse for a feeling of closeness and for a shiny coat; where you enjoyed a corn-husk bee and played tricks; where, out of the fiddle or accordian a waltz tune enlivened the atmosphere; where work-horses were led into shelter upon a sudden thunderstorm; where you saw a mother-mouse scurrying about to lead you away from her nestful of mousies ; where the barn swallow patched a mud-nest and chirped its cheery note; where pretty big girls played house when the hay-loft was empty; where we hid to cry out our woes; where we spread a robe on the hay for a noon-nap or a cowboy slept there overnight; where Pa blew out the lantern and hung it atop on a sturdy nail, as when he took time to talk to us; where Pa and his company stood by the open-barn door and talked stuff and Pa laughed and laughed! This was prairieland's barn!

During the winter months the pioneer man had to take down each harness that hung on the wooden holder on the stall-post ... as a set of harnesses belonged to a team of horses. Every horse needed a special fit, either for Jack or Querly, Mike or Lady, Nan or Jossie.

Each harness was brought separately into the warm kitchen where the repair work was done. Work bench, leather tools and appliances filled the kitchen to capacity. I can still smell it ... the horse sweat mixed with leather odor.

Somehow the condition of the harness matched the personality of the horse. An easy-going draft horse had very little wrong with his harness; a sprightly type, like Jossie was, ripped her harness in many places. Deep lines etched Pa's face as if the leather tools helped edge the hard task of fixing Jossie's mess of a harness. "She is a crazy horse," sighed Pa, "but what would I do without her at the gang plow?" A little bell tingled as Pa lifted the harness from one knee to the other, stitching and mending the unravels. Pa's workbench showed signs of rub. For many, many winter hours he shifted himself in and out, to reach for this tool or that harness needle.

As Pa grasped for leather-thread, he held it between his lips with no concern for the dirty taste. Gray suspenders held up his dirt-shiny, baggy pants. Close by, on the floor set a spittoon. He'd spit out the saliva-mixture of leather residue. I can still hear the zing-sound which the spittle made as it hit the mark ... fi-ew!

Pa was ordinarily neat about his habits. He never smoked nor chewed tobacco to my knowledge. His temper was easily aroused when there wasn't order, or when no common sense was used in any type of work. He had pity for a horse which suffered a neck-bruise from a wrong collar, but could get easily upset at horses' lack of obedience. He could be rough on his family and at other times have a deep concern especially when one was sick. He enjoyed reading the "Staats Anzeiger" and "Kirchenbote," as well as the German Bible. On occasion he would read an English article and sheepishly ask one of us girls what it was about.

As our parlor was filled with company Pa would be the entertainer. He would discuss Scripture and politics; he would tell folktales from the old country and move into Russian talk that sounded hilarious. You see he served in the Russo-Japanese War. He could tell jokes and laugh at his quip. The elders cherished the parlor and the young people played games in the kitchen.

Nothing pleased and touched Pa more than singing the old-time religious songs. He got us an organ. When Ed Kreins visited at the Neher home, Ed and Ludwig sang to their hearts' content ... Pa, bass and Ed, tenor. Soon Ottilia and I sang, as a duet, "Red River Valley," at one of the school programs. All in all, we had more time for the finer things in life.

Young people around the neighborhood made the bend of the Knife River a place of outdoor recreation. In the earlier days of fishing we made our own fishing poles. Even the hooks were made of safety pins and bait? — a tiny piece of salt pork attracted the fishes.

Net-fishing became a common Sunday afternoon activity, even an expeditious adventure, attracting more and more families. A couple of older boys acquired a net-imagination of maneuvering and meandering the net at specific places, giving it a quick jerky draw and coming out with a good supply of fishes.

The women folk brought huge bread loaves, homemade doughnuts or kuchen. The fishes were scraped, washed and dipped into seasoned flour and fried in a black, cast-iron pan where fresh lard was sizzling. It was heated on an open outdoor fire that flickered between a couple of prairie stones. A crispy, browned piece of fish was placed on a hunk of bread and passed out. No bother with plates except coffee mugs. Coffee was brewed on the grate. Even a stranger cowboy followed the whiff of aroma and joined the picnickers. These net-fishing fun times at the bend of the Knife River set the mode for pioneer fish stories.

Choke-cherry picking time? This was a family job. It wasn't only pailsful of the native fruit ... it was cream can and tubsful that had to be picked. An ordinary family put up gallons and gallons of choke-cherry jell.

Often we would take an entire weekday, or join neighbors on a Sunday choke-cherry-picking spree. Likely it could become a monotony. We had to wade and splash in the river and that not more kids drowned was a mystery. You either sank or you learned fast to keep afloat. No guards around either. Nature, in its force, created an unforeseen hole of obscure depth. A slip and slide and one went down resulting in hectic struggle. We never had swimming lessons and we never realized the danger.

Dams were a threat too. One Sunday afternoon the Martin girls joined us on an ice-skating frolic on our massive and deep dam. The ice broke and Emelia went down. The more we tried to help her get out the more the ice broke, and at the right moment someone pushed in a long board for Emilia to grab a hold of ... a fumbling of a rescue act. Here again the warmth of the Majestic stove was Emilia's first aid application. A guardian angel must have hovered over prairieland's children and waved his protective arms over them.

Along with daring ventures we dared something else. The three oldest of the Neher girls joined a group of the neighbors. Young people on a chug, chug truck drive to the north. One of the Martin boys drove the secondhand truck that Pa had had purchased. As we crossed the Knife River, Jack Crowley stopped us and speculated our aim. He guessed that we were on our way to Glitz, the fortune-teller, who lived a few miles north in a wretched sod hovel. Glitz was at the height of popularity since he was frequently sought to detect cattle or horse thieves. Word passed that he could look at the lines of one's palm and with the aid of a mysterious glass ball, he could tell our fortunes. He looked through it with quizzical eyes. His tiny silver specs, perched on the front of his nose and his shiny, bald head added to the weirdness.

One by one we sat on a creaky chair next to Glitz. As he studied our palm-lines and gazed into the fortune ball, I slid, out of fidgety, to a forward move, and into my seat penetrated a splint that stuck loose on the tattered chair. Ouch! At the same moment Glitz related my destiny lines. One capricious omen stood out ... that I would marry an ugly man! The sliver had a physical prick but the sting of such a forecast troubled me to no end. So were the fortunes of many others that Glitz prophesied. Each one had a demonic effect. Christ Opp just about went hay-wire. He dwelled on the omen so much that he had to be taken to Grandma Lennick for a "brauching"(spiritual meditation) to get the Glitz devil out of him.

The whole north country range was in an arousal. Carl Bauers brought the fortune-telling-news to our parents. They even told Ma and Pa that Matilda and Ottilia each paid Glitz a quarter for his services and Pauline, a dime. Pa took the razor strap ... stopped short and scolded, moreso for the money we gave Glitz and because we used our truck to haul the fortune-seekers. I said to Pa: "You can have my fortune!" Then Pa burst out laughing ... and we all laughed.

The truck became a regular focal point. Henry Fetzer, a hired man and a cousin, took each of us older girls on a learn-to-drive spree. But not Elsie. Quite dismayed, Elsie decided to learn by herself.

She drove it round and round in the yard and finally aimed at the summer kitchen, expecting the truck to halt by itself. She banged into the south wall, shoving it in so the wall rested nicely against the family table. Elsie just scolded and scolded.

At one of our Knife River maneuvers we got the truck stuck right in the middle of the river. Fred Martin dumped a pail of water straight to the front face of the truck and christened it "Glitz" --- and so Glitz, the truck, remained a distinguished symbol in the Neher yard, as Glitz, the fortune-teller, left a mark of doomsday for the whole north country.

The day the Neher truck was christened "Glitz"!

The Johannes "Gemeinde" (Congregation) folded up and the community's German families became members of the Congregational Church of Hebron.

During the early 1920's the whole Neher clan piled into a Model T Ford, meandering the country dirt roads, around and over hill and vale, eighteen miles to Hebron. Chuck-chuck-chuck, as Pa gave her the low and the farther on up the slower the car went. The load was too heavy. Elsie pushed herself in rhythm against the front seat, aiming to help along. At an ascending hill Pa would command the back-seat bunch to get out and walk up the hill. It took a couple of hours to get to Hebron with the open-sided car that bucked the wind. During drizzling weather Pa would snap on the side-flaps, then the spit-curl hair-dos stayed in better shape.

As was the fashion, waved and spit-curls were in style. On a Saturday Ottilia would boil up flax seed with water and use the slime to set the hair-design. To tell the truth, among the whole row of Sunday-school kids, Ottilia's head stood out.

The whole family attended Sunday-school, worship services as well as prayer meetings that were held in the afternoon. The pioneer parents meant business with church attendance. It was deemed a holy duty for parents to give the children spiritual nurture in the German language. So insistent that the German Bible and hymns be used that "third degree" force was practiced. Gradually antagonism entered all German-oriented churches and affliction became the rule for the movement; that is, the change from the German to English.

During snow-drifted roads, Pa would hitch Lady and Mike, a spirited team, to a sled that contained hay, robes and heated stones and pack the oldest girls into the sled. Pa sat/stood in front, dressed in heavy coat-wear, and giddy-yapped the horses on an eighteen-mile sleigh trek to one of Hebron's many churches for a Christmas Eve program. We would stay the night at the home of Aunt Matilda Gaertner and eat of her delicious borscht and Christmas kolache. We recited our pieces with elation and endured the long drives with anticipation. Ma had the chores done and the house warm. Ordeals? No! They weren't hardships!

PAULINE NEHER
DICKINSON NORMAL SCHOOL GRADUATE

The Dirty Thirties
Prairie's Salutation

During the course of Elm Creek country school years a good number of pupils graduated from the eighth grade and went on to higher learning and vocational schools. Others stayed on family farms and sought their future on the land.

Country schools turned out citizens who went out into the world with a will to work. Children grew up with strong ties to the soil and to their churches. They were given a groundwork to their heritage. They were the children of tough upbringing and were taught not to be wasteful nor extravagant, to not buy anything unless you could pay for it and to be content with the simple necessities of life. Daughters were admonished to marry the young man of whom parents approved and who definitely must be of the same faith. She must not come home, pregnant, or she'd be disowned and not allowed into the home ever again.

The son, likewise, was to place his choice for a wife on a girl with good physical build, so she'd be able to pitch in with any kind of farm labor and that she be subject to their son; and if, by chance, the newlyweds farm the old man's land, they must do as he says, or else!

In Neher's family, upbringing was no different. The girls were getting to be maidens. On the whole, the Neher girls, as well as other grown girls, knew very little of intimacy. Nothing of menses nor sexual relationships was ever mentioned to daughters. It was considered dirty. Girls were more or less shocked into reality ... and punished when things went wrong. Let's face it, we were all uninformed ... too much so.

Both Pa and Ma kept close eye on Matilda's boy relationship intents ... as well as on Tillie. Many arguments resulted until the talked-into marriages were set by our parents. As for me, I attended two years of high school in Hebron and then transferred to Dickinson Normal School where I received the extent of my education.

My Normal School days weren't all roses ... there were lots of thorns that pricked me along the way.

The lack of clothes and eats were my primary needs. I went baby-sitting for a quarter a night to a south-side Dickinson home. One night the man of the house left the dance hall and came to his home, attacking me for a rape. I struggled out of his grasp and started running at a gasping pace across the tracks to my cold aparment. The villain ran after me but could not catch up. I could outrun most anybody, which was a feat all my life. I'd win every race July 4th celebrations and at church picnics. However, the greatest compensation of my running skill paid off on that Winter's night of long ago ... a young girl's shock!

I happened to be a home economics student. Miss Poole was the instructor, and manager of the college cafe as well. One day she asked me what I had for dinner. "A candy bar," I answered. She soon realized my state of poorness and offered me work in the cafe for one hour to earn a quarter's worth of food for my noon meal. What a piece of mission! I had eats and training as well. The cafeteria meal kept me from starving.

It took me four quarters to complete high school and receive a secretarial certificate. To honor the graduates, Miss Poole sponsored a "tea". Again Miss Poole asked one college girl to lend Pauline Neher a black chiffon dress to wear to the tea. It was too big, but Oh, how big I felt! These were hard times, yet good times!

At the Neher farm adverse conditions took over. The crop was very poor. Pa was struck by a lightning bolt and hovered in poor health for some time. After regaining strength he hitched up three horses, Bess, Mike and Lady, to a load of wheat, so to haul it to the mill in Hebron for conversion into flour for Winter's supply. As Pa jumped off of the wagon Lady kicked and knocked him out. As a result he laid in bed at the Peter Fehr home as an invalid for weeks. This too was very hard on Ma, and she, too, was failing in health. Gradually the family members went their separate ways. Elsie, Edwin and Anne settled near the west coast, and Matilda, Ottilia, Louise and myself sought our destinies in North Dakota. Changes were evident!

The years of despair were upon us ... over the whole country! It did not rain. The hot sun scorched everything. By 1935 many families had left their farms and moved west. Others talked about leaving but didn't. The farms were their life's assets. They worked very hard for it ... the Nehers as well. So they stayed!

The drouth struck ... year after year, worse than the last year. Hardly anything to wear and nothing to eat—just plain nothing except grasshoppers. They ate everything ... they even started eating the buildings.

Pa lost two quarters of land to taxes and desperately tried to hang on to the homestead and the surrounding land, but tragedy hit him threefold. Ma never regained her health. She became irresponsible and had to be confined for the rest of her life. Pa gave the farm management over to Edwin and he moved to Beulah and became a day laborer at planting trees and doing carpentry work.

Edwin was single. Another couple lived with him and they boarded the school teacher who was a homosexual. In the absence of Edwin he started a fire on the large barn that included 31 head of cattle, three horses, hay, feed, harnesses ... everything burned to a total loss. Pa cried in deepest lament and hurt as he gazed upon the seared carcasses of the beloved horses and cows!

This was the end of any claim to prairieland's farmstead or homestead gain ... despite the years of tortuous work, everything was gone for the Nehers!

But was everything a goner? In the material realm, yes! In the sensual and spiritual realm, no!

Pa went back to his Mother's faith ... a conversion to a Baptist! He became active in Beulah's Baptist Church as a witness of God's bounty, in things that had eternal value. "What has the world to offer? Nothing lasting! Only the benefits of the Creator's land and hard work, mixed with joys thereof!" Pa would say.

Our pioneer father was touched by a mellowness that we all felt. At his funeral service his favorite hymn was sung: "It is well with my soul ... it is well!"

THE NEHER GIRLS

Edwin Neher and his finance Esther having a good time with a friend and two of Edwin's sisters.

THE DIEDE FAMILY

After my school sojourn at Dickinson, ND, and having spent one more year on the Neher farm, I fully realized I wanted a life on the open prairies. No city life for me.
Having had the Glitz prediction that I'd marry an ugly man I made sure I'd court a good-looking guy. And that Jake Diede was! A second Clark Gable, especially when he sported a well-trimmed little mustache. I married him and we lived in with his parents and younger sister, on the Henry Diede farm ... a few miles southeast of the famous butte, Custer Lookout. It was called the Antelope Community. A beautiful farming area, close neighbors and good country schools. Proud people lived here.
I was especially welcomed by Aunt Lyd Diede and Aunt Ann Diede, who were the instigators for community life and the charters of Lookout Homemakers Club. Here I began a 50-year homemaker-extension-work tenure. It was an educational program which I thoroughly enjoyed.
A young married couple living in with parents or in-laws has been a policy that was brought over from the old country. It spells no good for any couple; and neither was it good for Jake and me. I soon sensed our differences in philosophy, in intellect as well as in spiritual matters. I wasn't able to be myself, however, my mother-in-law (Groszmutter Diede) was kind to me and taught me many a cooking/baking lesson.
After nearly two years the Henry Diedes moved to Hebron. A beautiful child, Darlayne Mae, was born. She brought due love and life into the family circle. She sang a Christmas carol solo at a church program when she was three years old. She took solo parts throughout grade and high school activities and sang 'The Lord's Prayer' as Miss Hebron in the

1952 State Beauty contest. Today Darlayne Buchli is employed as an R.N. at a Medical Clinic in Rapid City, SD, and serves in her church gloryfying God with her beautiful voice and her vivacious personality. She and her husband Myron have raised four sons.

Audrey Faith, the second daughter, became Darlayne's little sister. This child, too, was filled with talent. She was a leader. In school her classmates relied on Audrey for critical answers. Involved in a wide curriculum she thoroughly enjoyed cheerleading. She rated as valedictorian in both high school and college commmencements.

Audrey Diede was chosen as Miss Dickinson in the 1963 State Beauty contest and with an added sweep of Miss Congeniality and Miss Talent. Audrey Williamson resides in Denver and teaches in special education, serves in church affairs and leads an active family life with her husband Jim and their two sons.

Rodney J., our youngest, earned his Eagle Scout Award and fared well in the sports pursuit in high school as well as in college.

Rod Diede was elected 1964 Homecoming Chief of Dickinson State College. He taught and coached in high schools and served as principal in Bowman, ND, schools. Several years ago he joined the Dakota Western Bank staff and acts as vice president of that bank. He's active in his church council and serves on the city commission. He has acquired two Master's degrees in administration and banking, and resides with his family in Bowman, ND.

These are productive citizens ... our adult children!

With no meaning for boast, our children have grown up in the American rights where opportunities were open and worship is free.

We were no perfect family ... by no means.

The denial of human rights sauntered yet strongly in our family as well as many other families. A communal trace.

Here is where the word "ugly" took prevalent in our family and where 'Glitz' touched a bit right ... not in looks, nor in works, but in the enforcement of denying the woman any rights ... especially in money matters. Jake and I have had strong differences and it was hard on the children. I'm sorry. Any movement for a change is hard.

Relationship purgatory? Yes!

But out of it is sprouting a stronger family relationship as well as a respect for each other's individuality.

I firmly advocate that America stands for challenging creative living ... therefore I'm compelled to write!

Hold high the torch!
You did not light its glow -
'Twas the Author Above, you know
It started as you sat on a prairie-stone
The Creator spoke and you were not alone ...
Why sigh? The prairieland trusteth me!
And in that instant He set me free
To tell the story and write it out -
Hold high the torch! To all I'll shout!

by Pauline Neher Diede

S I N C E R E L Y   Y O U R S !

Listen! What would it mean to the heart of the world __
    If the Prairieland epoch of it goodness was told?
In hiking about I watch the birds take to flight __
    Soaring heaven's blue sky ... what a view of a sight!
Here-a-bouts was a nest, many decades ago __
    Into the open-mouthed birdie, a crumb I'd throw!
Yonder on a fence post ... a little over the hill __
    The meadowlark's clear song, a bird's sweet trill;
I leant my ear and felt the melody in my heart __
    A child's happy way ... every morning a stirring new start!
           __as when The Prairie Was Home!

I slept in a hovel that was crowded and filled __
    The prairie-land acres which Uncle Sam had willed;
Pa broke its sod .. staggered in a rectangular form __
    Thus borne four more babies without thought or alarm;
The jointed stone/sod hut had to do for a house __
    What noise and carouse ... I was a specie of a louse;
Looking out the trite window I crept unto the sill __
    O wishful star! I long to run the freedom's hill;
Where the gopher perks up ... lynching on to a calf's tail __
    Quite so! Romping o'er the rocks, like the wind we'd sail!
           __as when The Prairie Was Home!

Thus we moved a-ways north on the Bitterman place __
    Homesick for the sod-house, in confusion I did race;
Instructed to a course as when work was the deal __
    The gut of the prairie ... the proof that life was real!
Hiding by the play-hill, the pity --- one's self to lose __
    Running along a rabbit's trail, I beckoned to choose;
Horizon's butte so weirdly far and yet so near __
    Thundering clouds and lightning bolt so fast did appear;
Its ravage hit close, out the north window we'd look __
    Oh, to dwell by the sod-sure wall ... such a fear-free nook!
           __as when The Prairie Was Home!

The young one's work ... herding the cows, orders were such ___
    Around the Deep Creek, on Scheck, keeping vigilant watch!
As the time came for school, ó'er the prairies we'd tread ___
    Obey the language rule ... and do what parents had said;
Such turmoil, of, what's right? The school kids did suffer ___
    Yet on the whole country schools had much to offer!
The dug-outs proof ... sustain on the open prairieland ___
    The sod-made dwellings at its generation did stand!
When life was a school ... too hard were the working days ___
    Oh, for the time fo return, to a prairie's pomp-ways!
          ___as when The Prairie Was Home!

Elm Creek's prairie-land ... close to the Knife River bend ___
    God, the Creator, forever, His goodness doth send!
In all its simplicity we stand awed and serene ___
    Listen to the land! Open ye eyes, to behold the scene!
The lesson of its story .. enhances wisdom's worth ___
    The Giver of all things ... the fruits of the good earth!
Listen to the land as Nature echoes her yelp ___
    We look unto the hills from whence cometh our help!
Oh, Creator-God, in all thine majesty and might ___
    To Prairie's paradise, we greet with love and delight!
          ___as when The Prairie Was Home!

        Sincerely yours,
        Pauline Neher Diede

THE SALUTATION

THE ELM CREEK/KNIFE RIVER COUNTRY

The Elm Creek/Knife River country is receiving due recognition through the book: The Prairie Was Home!

This mite country of southwest Mercer County, North Dakota, represents the ordinary expanse of prairie hills and sloping vales ... indicative of a Plains States region.

Commonly speaking not much is being said nor written about the prairieland, perhaps because of its ordinariness and its simplicity.

It's time we take a keener interest in the stand of a common land which our forebears homesteaded and trusted it for survival;

It's time we assess the importance of its productivity and contribution toward world hunger;

It's time we breathe in its pure, fresh air and enjoy Nature's wholesome and healthful ways of life;

It's time we behold the sunrise and sunset grandeurs and listen to the hills' messages;

It's time we accept the goodness of this land-of-simplicity with heart-felt gratification;

It's time we heed the conservation measures that President Theodore Roosevelt so vigorously ordained;

It's time we hallow America's scenic and historical resources as well as value the plain and ordinary country;

It's time we confess that the book: The Prairie Was Home was the inspired writing ...a mission at that !!

— Pauline Neher Diede

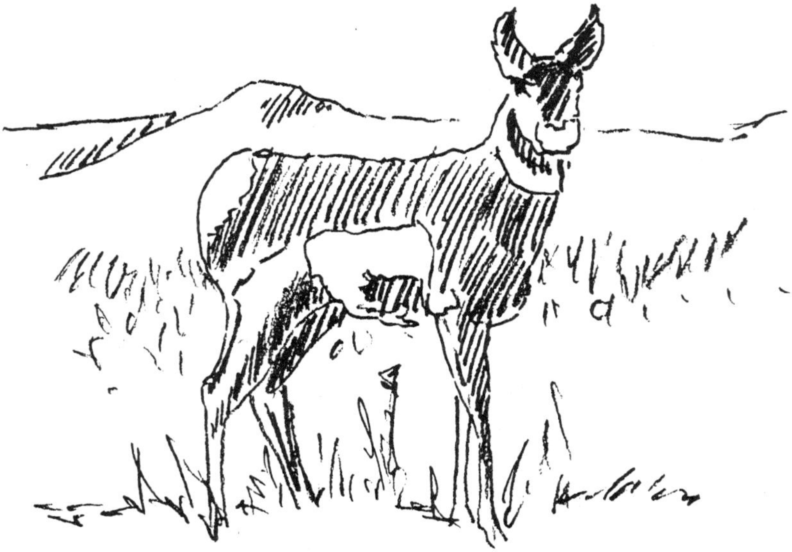